P. 97

Mendelssohn

THE MEN
BEHIND THE MUSIC

THE MEN BEHIND THE MUSIC

Edited by
C. HENRY WARREN

KENNIKAT PRESS
Port Washington, N. Y./London

These sixteen biographical interpretations of famous composers originally appeared in *The Radio Times*, to the Editor of which I am indebted for permission to reprint them.

C.H.W.

THE MEN BEHIND THE MUSIC

First published in 1931
Reissued in 1970 by Kennikat Press
Library of Congress Catalog Card No: 74-102844
SBN 8046-0766-4

Manufactured by Taylor Publishing Company   Dallas, Texas

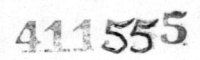

CONTENTS

		PAGE
I	J. S. BACH	1
	By FILSON YOUNG	
II	BEETHOVEN	10
	By H. N. BRAILSFORD	
III	HECTOR BERLIOZ	21
	By WILFRID ROOKE-LEY	
IV	BRAHMS	31
	By RICHARD CHURCH	
V	CHOPIN	41
	By WINIFRED HOLTBY	
VI	HANDEL	51
	By C. HENRY WARREN	
VII	HAYDN	61
	By WILFRID ROOKE-LEY	
VIII	LISZT	71
	By FRANCIS BRETTARGH	
IX	MOZART	82
	By J. C. SQUIRE	
X	MENDELSSOHN	90
	By SACHEVERELL SITWELL	

CONTENTS

		PAGE
XI	MUSSORGSKY	99
	By C. Henry Warren	
XII	SCHUBERT	109
	By J. W. N. Sullivan	
XIII	TCHAIKOVSKY	117
	By John Mann	
XIV	VERDI	128
	By Hermon Ould	
XV	WAGNER	137
	By Richard Church	
XVI	WEBER	147
	By Francis Brettargh	

THE MEN BEHIND THE MUSIC

I

J. S. BACH

By FILSON YOUNG

THE genius of Johann Sebastian Bach was no accidental freak of nature. If ever there was a case of hereditary development and of the slow ripening of genius through successive generations (which is what we expect of, but seldom get from, nature) it was the case of Bach. For five generations and almost one hundred years his ancestors had filled Thuringia with music, and he himself was the fifth generation of a race that was undoubtedly specially gifted in the practice of music as an art and profession. Bach himself was the culmination and fine flower of this great blossoming. He had nineteen children, not all of whom survived childhood; but those who did were all musicians. Nevertheless, the great climax had been reached in him; although one at least of his sons added genius and distinction that in quality approached his own, the great efflorescence of genius began to die away; and after reaching this mighty culmination, it ebbed again until, in the year 1840, the last representative of this great clan vanished from the earth. As in a natural vegetation, beginning with shoots and saplings that grow and spread through the centuries, until some giant of the forest overtops the rest in grandeur, so degeneration and decay set in, the last giant vanishes, and the wind brushes the bare downland where once it roared in the branches and sang in the forest leaves.

Something as striking and as complete as what happened in the case of his family and race has happened to the memory and understanding of Bach. During his lifetime he had a great reputation and prestige in the part of Germany where he lived, although he had no particular fame beyond its narrow bounds. The amazing body of work which was to be his legacy to the world of music was unknown and unsuspected in his time ; hardly any music of his was published in his lifetime ; masterpieces were written for some occasion, performed on it, and put away and forgotten. Priceless manuscripts of his lay about in cupboards at St. Thomas's School at Leipzig, or were used to wrap up parcels. He was undoubtedly a great man in his own time and place, but when he died, it did not seem that so local a fame would endure ; in fact, it did not. By the time the last of his pupils had died, his name and memory seemed to have passed almost into oblivion ; his very grave was unknown.

And then something began to happen. The seed that had lain so long in the soil was not dead, but germinating. Here and there compositions of Bach's were discovered and their genius recognized. People began to collect his music and manuscripts ; and, incredible as it may appear, and overwhelming as were the chances against the preservation of even a small part of his music, it began to be recovered, studied, and its amazing genius recognized. One by one masterpieces were rediscovered in this collection and that ; a great society was formed for the editing and collecting of his works ; and to-day, after a period of complete oblivion, the world possesses a tremendous treasure in his collected works—perhaps the greatest treasure of one man's art known to the world.

A good deal has been lost, but what remains is as remarkable in its quality as it is overwhelming in its extent. Just the work of an honest, industrious labourer whose genius for hard work was as great as his genius for art—just that and no more has given the world this priceless treasure ; and the man who would have been most astonished —for he never took any steps to preserve his work or give it to the world at large—would have been Sebastian Bach himself.

This great process of the reblossoming of Bach's genius is not yet complete ; it is happening in our own time. I remember, when I was a child, being first made aware of the grandeur of his work ; it was then really only understood by comparatively few people who had definitely cultivated music and were intimate with its language. To play a Bach fugue in a drawing-room was then regarded as a somewhat eccentric and highbrow proceeding ; to appear to like it was almost an affectation. To-day Bach is the possession of the common people all over the Western world. In England in the last years he has gradually become a really popular composer ; and he whose works were unheard and neglected a hundred years ago is to-day one of the world's 'best sellers' in music. The whole thing is like a myth; it seems incredible that there ever was such a person.

The recovery of his music has had a strangely physical coincidence in the recovery of his body. It was known that he had been buried in St. John's Church, and somewhat hazy tradition placed his unmarked grave somewhere near the south door of the church; but it was not until 1894 that a remarkable discovery was made when excavations for new foundations were being made in the churchyard. The sexton's receipt of the year 1750 showed that Bach had been buried in an oak coffin, and 150 years later, when these repairs were being made, three, and only three, oak coffins were discovered on the site that tradition had assigned as his burial place. In the year of his death, out of fourteen hundred persons who were buried in that place, only twelve were buried in oak coffins; hence the importance of this discovery. In one of the three were the bones of a young woman, in another the skeleton of a child, and in the third the skeleton of an elderly man, the skull of which exhibited at first glance the characteristic features that one would have expected from the two portraits in existence of Bach. After copious researches had been made into the relation of the fleshy parts of the face to the bony parts in elderly people, so that the line of the skin over the line of the bones could be approximately indicated, a Leipzig sculptor, Seffner, succeeded in modelling on a plaster cast the features which, when compared with the contemporary portraits of Bach, showed an appreciable likeness. The authenticity of the remains was thus placed beyond doubt, so that even a physical resurrection was achieved after the reblossoming of the artistic genius that had lain undiscovered so long.

There is to me something extremely noble and touching in this story of so narrow a triumph over time, and of the human spirit snatching its beloved from out the sunless oblivion that had so nearly engulfed it. Once more had Life triumphed over Time and Death.

Can we pluck the curtain a little farther back and look into the face of this almost mythical person, and see what manner of man he was? The face in his portraits is, superficially, strangely unattractive, stern, and even hard. From its strange environment of wig it looks out upon us with an unfamiliar, almost unfriendly regard; seamed with lines of resolution, of endurance, even of suffering; unrelieved by any suggestion of kindness and humour. Yet we know enough of him to be aware that kindness and humour were a very definite part of his make-up, and that his chief faults were irritability and a quite definite inability to maintain discipline among his subordinates. There is but one thing that can even seem to account for the prodigious volume and genius of his achievement—that he worked hard every day of his life. 'Anyone could do what I have done', he wrote, naively, 'who works as hard as I have worked.' Bach was probably the least self-conscious genius who ever lived. He never sat down to compose a masterpiece, but the most trivial thing that he happened to do in the routine of his work *was* a masterpiece; he could not help it. Like the blossoming tree shaken by the wind, he had but to stir himself to shower forth music. Hence the mythical and stupendous story of an apparently commonplace man working daily at his commonplace tasks; his work, once done, put away, tidied up, finished with, utterly swallowed up in the gulf of oblivion; and a century later breaking forth on the world with all the glory and freshness of a summer dawn.

There is so little known about Bach, so little on record either in his own writings or in the writing of any contemporary, that we are thrown back to the study of his work itself before we can have any sense of intimacy with him, or feel that we know really what he was like. The known facts about his life could be written on a sheet of notepaper; but study, record, and commentary on his work might well fill volumes and volumes. One of the influences which undoubtedly delayed the world's appreciation of Bach was the extraordinary vogue of his great contemporary, Handel. Both were great men in their day; but whereas appreciation of Bach's greatness was limited to the people in his own environment and to the musicians who had met him and heard him play, Handel's fame was spread far and wide over England and Germany in his own lifetime. In fact, he may be said to have administered a kind of 'knock-out blow' to music which arrested its growth for well-nigh a hundred years. Musical England became dominated by the *Messiah* and remained so for years, while the *B Minor* and the *St Matthew Passion* lay unseen and unsung. The vogue of the *Messiah* and of Handel's other oratorios diverted English music very largely into the channel of oratorio in which it kept its narrow and monotonous way for many a year.

Thus a comparison between Bach and Handel becomes inevitable; both are great men, and at their highest and best they attain to a region where there is no competition or comparison. But as they themselves recede, and as their music becomes more and more studied, Handel somewhat diminishes in stature, while Bach looms ever larger. They were, indeed, profoundly different in temperament, and the difference is reflected in their music. Where Handel was almost always dramatic, Bach was almost always emotional. Handel painted in broad splashes of colour; Bach drew in long interwoven outlines. Where Handel was a Reubens, Bach was a Titian. He had in him something of the nature of Albrecht Dürer and of Blake. Handel derived much of his inspiration from the English language—Milton and the English Bible. Bach, except in the case of the Passions, had little verbal inspiration, save what could be derived from German hymns; the text of the cantatas is for the most part sadly inadequate to the magnificent musical structure to which they were fitted. It is almost impossible to think of Bach writing anything at once so simple, so thrillingly dramatic and so utterly magnificent as the chorus ' Then round about the starry Throne ' from Handel's *Samson*. But then it is equally impossible to think of Handel having written anything at once so poignant, so touching and so architecturally expressive as the first and last choruses from the *St Matthew Passion*.

And when we come to look at the technical idiom in which each expressed himself, we find again a similarity only superficial and apparent, a difference intrinsic and profound. They both wrote fugues and suites because those were contemporary forms in which composers of the day expressed themselves; but there the likeness ends. Handel, for all his greatness, is a ' dated ' composer; his is the music, exquisite and magnificent, of a period. Bach's is the music of all time. There is no harmony, no dissonance, no chord in the whole range of music from the earliest mediaeval plainsong to the latest devices of a Debussy or a Delius which is not to be found in Bach. One would almost dare to say that all that there ever was in music, and all that there ever will be, is in some sense included or anticipated by Bach.

It is for that reason that his work continues to be a living and ever richer study, instead of being merely the subject of antiquarian research. That is why Bach grows ever fresher and more popular as his music becomes more and more a possession of the people. As I said at the beginning of this article, that process is still going on. Listeners to British broadcasting are unusually fortunate in that they are assisting in the work of unfolding for the first time to English listeners the great and the lovely content of the Church Cantatas. A few pioneers, notably Sir Hugh Allen and Sir Hubert Parry, made something like a complete study and presentation of these works; but their performances were necessarily confined to a limited and localized public. It would not be possible, indeed, for any organization, except one with the resources of the B.B.C., to attempt to give with anything like adequacy the whole of these cantatas to the public. When you consider that there are nearly two hundred of them, that they require an orchestra of extremely skilful players, an organ of the right pitch, a small but highly-trained chorus, and a body of soloists who have studied and acquired the art of singing the music in the peculiar style which it demands, you will see how extravagant are the resources required for a performance that lasts, on an average, twenty minutes for each cantata. Mr. Ernest Newman, referring to these performances of the B.B.C., described them as 'the greatest gift ever made to English music'. Yet they are only a part—although hitherto an almost unexplored part—of the vast treasures that lie waiting, not so much to be discovered by the expert (for he has discovered them) as to be given to the public. By 'given' I mean so performed, and so frequently performed, as to become familiar to the listening public. Until this has been done and this music strikes not strangely, but familiarly, on the ear of the man in the street—not until then can we say that as a nation we really possess the art of Sebastian Bach.

II
BEETHOVEN
By H. N. BRAILSFORD

ONE may be too curious about the life of a great artist. We enjoy the verbal music of *Adonais* no better after prying into Shelley's dealings with Harriet. One can learn everything about him from Maurois' *Ariel*, save that he was a poet and a thinker. But there is a case for informing ourselves about Beethoven's personality. The poet can convey in words all we need to know about his opinions. The musician does not tell us how he viewed life: what he expresses is at most the emotion which he felt, as he pondered and struggled. Yet Beethoven had strong opinions. It was a daring thing for a composer writing within reach of the Austrian police to dedicate a symphony to Napoleon. Not only did Beethoven write the Eroica in honour of the first Consul: he tore up his dedication when his hero proclaimed himself Emperor. His opinions, then, had some bearing on his music: a political enthusiasm stimulated the first of his works which deserves to be called not merely beautiful but great.

There is another reason which drives lovers of Beethoven's music to study his life. Few artists grow so visibly as we survey their work in the order of its composition. The development of his technique is not a sufficient explanation; certainly in that respect he never ceased to invent. He is constantly winning freedom within the traditional forms and rules, which at last he bursts and breaks, modulating from one key to another with increasing subtlety and audacity, and discovering fresh colours in his orchestral instruments. So much, in some measure, one may say of every original artist. But in Beethoven's case one feels that the man is growing as noticeably as the composer. If he had died in 1804, his early work would have ranked him in quality, though not in quantity, with Haydn and Mozart. The world had heard few symphonies as lovely and interesting as his First and Second. Yet when he came to his Third (the Eroica) we feel that something has happened to this composer. By taking thought he has added many cubits to his stature. For the first time we call him not only a great artist but a great man. The early works were beautiful patterns of sound, but this symphony reflects the experience of a man who by suffering and struggle had won his right to hope and believe.

Ludwig von Beethoven was born in 1770 at Bonn, amid the beauties of the Rhine Valley. His grandfather, a Fleming, was a chorister in the service of the Archbishop-Elector, an enlightened patron of music, and rose to be conductor of his concerts. His father, who sang in the same choir, had a narrower mind and a harsher character, and his drunken habits brought the family to squalid poverty. To his mother, of whom we know too little, Beethoven was deeply attached, but she died before he was eighteen. The father, who wished to exploit Ludwig as an infant-prodigy, neglected his general education, kept him hard at work at fiddle and piano, and published his childish compositions with falsified dates. His growth, when one compares him with Mozart, was slow; yet at seventeen, on a brief visit to Vienna, he won high praise from that brilliant genius. He was well grounded in Bach, played the organ as well as the piano, and gained valuable experience as viola-player in the Elector's orchestra. While still in his teens he was obliged to take over from his drunken father the responsibility for the household. Encouraged by Haydn, during a visit to Bonn, he sought his fortune, in 1792, in the imperial city of Vienna, at this time the musical capital of Europe. Here he took lessons in composition from Haydn, but the self-willed, though hard-working, pupil was too tactless to retain a teacher's regard. As a pianist, however, he made his way rapidly, chiefly by his gift of improvization. At his concerts someone would suggest a theme, and on this, abandoning himself to a fury of creation, he would pour forth variations which astonished his hearers as much by their prodigal invention as by the sure architecture of their form. But he was not at this time a popular figure in musical society. His contemporaries describe him as an ugly, but sturdy little man, with a shock of insurgent black hair. His manners were awkward, his accent provincial. To awkward manners, a provincial accent, and slovenly dress, he added a prickly and defiant independence. Mozart had worn a livery, and dined in the servants' hall of his patron. No man ever dared to treat Beethoven as less than an equal. Throughout life he was a democrat, formed by the French Revolution. A bust of the regicide, Brutus, stood on his bureau. When his brother, John, a war-profiteer, described himself on his visiting card as 'landowner', Beethoven retaliated by scribbling under his own name 'brain-owner'. On a visit to Goethe he horrified that courtier of genius by remaining covered and erect when they met the Imperial Family in the road. To the Archduke Karl, the commander of the European coalition against France, he wrote a dignified letter exhorting him to lead a movement for peace. His religious opinions were as unorthodox as his politics. No one who listens to the sublime choruses of the Ninth Symphony, or to the Convalescent's Hymn of Thanksgiving in the A Minor Quartette (Op. 131), can doubt that he was, emotionally, a deeply religious man. But his faith was pantheistic, and on one occasion the police even thought of prosecuting him for blasphemy based on some rash words spoken in a café.

At thirty, this young man had achieved success. Good judges considered him the first pianist of the day, and his compositions were spreading his fame as far as London. To our ears, these early works seem to place him in the school of Haydn and Mozart, but his contemporaries, even at times the great Haydn himself, thought them daring. Haydn, after all, belonged to the age of Sterne and Goldsmith; Beethoven to that of Byron and Goethe. But this successful man was deeply unhappy. At the age of twenty-six the first symptoms of deafness appeared. It is probable that the disease began in infancy, and it may have been congenital. Inexorably, though gradually, the curse crept upon him, and neither physicians nor quacks could relieve it. Partly from pride, partly from concern for his professional reputation, he concealed it even from his friends, and though he suffered agony from loneliness, he shunned society, until the world came to think him a misanthrope and a bear. Yet his was an affectionate and sociable nature, capable of gaiety as boisterous as his scherzos. Tones he could always hear better than words. He played in public for the last time in 1814, but in his later years his attempts to conduct brought humiliating disaster, and on the rare occasions when he played for friends, his fingers in the quieter passages would run over the keys and give no audible sound. The world could now reach him only by writing in the notebook which he always carried. At his last concert, in 1825, the great audience, listening for the first time to the Ninth Symphony, abandoned itself to a tempest of applause. His friends had to turn him round to see the clapping.

This curse, the most terrible which could visit a musician, was through thirty years the central fact of his life. The man reached greatness by defying it. In 1802, after a summer spent in vain in the rural quiet of Heiligenstadt, his hopes of a cure faded. In his will he described the despair and isolation of these years. Cut off from friendship and love, only his music remained, and for how long would he be able to create inaudible beauty? He even meditated suicide. Gradually his will asserted itself: he would fight; he would live to create. He ceases about this time to be ashamed of his affliction, and returns to society and finds that his work has gained. It is this victory which explains the sudden growth of power of which one is aware in the Eroica. It was dedicated to Napoleon, but does it not sing the new ideal of heroism? The death which the Funeral March celebrates is not that literal death of the body which the registrar records. It is rather the spiritual tomb from which a hero must escape. As one listens to the gay Scherzo and the triumphant Finale which follows it, instinctively one's inner voice repeats: 'And the third day he rose again.'

From this year onwards, this theme inspires all Beethoven's greater work. Occasionally one hears a note of resignation, but much more often of triumph. No man has written music of such abandoned gaiety. But there is the force of a titanic will in these terrific hymns to joy. They are not, like Mozart's, the outpourings of a child of nature. One is the witness of inner struggles in most of his loveliest creations; in the Fifth Symphony, and even in the Seventh, in the Violin Concerto, and even in the 'Emperor' Concerto, and most audibly one hears them in the third of the 'Razoumowsky' quartettes. If Beethoven inspires veneration as well as admiration, it is because one divines the depths and complexity of the experience behind those shapely and harmonious patterns of sound. This music of the mature middle period had an amplitude of scale, a dignity, and also an emotional complexity to which, as yet, the world had been a stranger.

There are few external events to record during this middle period, which stretches, more or less, from the Third Symphony to the Eighth (1804-1816). His life was devoted to incessant creation, varied only by his few concerts and by still rarer visits to Berlin or Budapest. There were two Beethovens, the creator and his keeper. This keeper was painfully inefficient. He lived an untidy, irregular existence in rooms that were a litter of papers, broken chairs, and unfinished meals. He was unbusinesslike over money, could not manage servants, and changed his lodgings almost every year. The most one can say for him is that he had the sense to take his charge into the country through the long summer months. There, in solitude, amid the lovely scenery which lies so near Vienna, Beethoven revelled in the woods, washed himself in the brooks from the dust of his battles, and heard as rhythm the contours of the hills. Most of his themes came to him out of doors. The keeper may have been a tragic man, at the sight of whose face, set in a mould of hopeless suffering, his friends could hardly refrain from tears. The creator could lose himself, a man intoxicated with joy, in his inner world of inaudible sound. Peasants would watch him in the fields, gesticulating madly, shouting, singing, beating time, and then stopping to jot down his themes in a notebook. Their cattle would stampede at the strange apparition, but it was deaf to their indignant shouts. The accounts of Beethoven's manner in conducting give the same impression of complete absorption in his music. To indicate a *diminuendo*, he would sink down until he disappeared behind the desk; for a *crescendo* he would rise very gradually, until at *fortissimo* he leapt into the air, shouting a strange, inarticulate cry. It is probable that no human being has lived for so many hours of every day in an inner world of sound. It became for him the real world, and of this world he was the emperor and the master.

Two sources of inspiration Beethoven had outside his music. First, there was his love of nature, legible most clearly in the Pastoral Symphony. One is surprised by his naive imitation of the brook and the birds, and one is tempted to say to him what Robert Bridges said to the nightingales: ' Beautiful must be the mountains whence ye come'. And then one recollects that long years had passed since he had heard the shout of a cuckoo or the rhythm of a brook.

> ' Nay, barren are those mountains and spent the streams;
> Our song is the voice of desire, that haunts our dreams.'

The other inspiration was love. But it was rather the hope of love that inspired him than any actual experience. One woman whom he loved wrote of his ' virginal purity '. He desired marriage, but always some impediment, his deafness, his poverty, his humble birth, or perhaps his modesty, stood in the way. Some brief happiness he may have had with the Countess Julia Guicciardi, and he wrote the Moonlight Sonata under its influence, but this pretty young woman preferred to marry a title. To the Countess Thérèsa of Brunswick, 'the immortal beloved' of his letters, he came nearer, at least in affectionate friendship, but though in some sense she loved him, they did not marry. To this attachment we owe the radiant Fourth Symphony, with its excited Finale, which seems to describe the entry of need and startling beauty into his life. His craving for love went unsatisfied to the end, and the saddest chapter is that which tells of his guardianship of his nephew, Karl. On this worthless youth, who wasted his own time and his uncle's slender earnings on billiards and women, and failed in every profession which he tried to enter, Beethoven lavished the pent-up affections of his lonely life. Karl could not stand the emotional strain of the relationship and made a half-hearted attempt at suicide.

Amid these shadows, lonely, embarrassed, and impoverished, in wretched health, and harassed by the worry and tragedy of Karl, Beethoven wrote the sublimest works of his career. For his third period includes the Ninth Symphony, the solemn Mass in D, and the five late string quartettes. He was at last ready to say all that was in him, and with turbulent majesty this man, who had travelled through all the circles of hell, wrote to Schiller's words his final Hymn to Joy. Who can doubt that the entire symphony was for Beethoven a revelation of the meaning of life; a celebration of the joy, which by love, but also by struggle, an emancipated humanity may attain? That music has this power of revelation he once declared to Bettina Brentano, Goethe's fascinating friend, though she may have polished the phrases which she professes to report. 'Music', he told her, 'is a higher revelation than all wisdom and philosophy'; indeed, it is 'the one incorporeal entrance into the higher world of knowledge'.

More intimately still, in the late quartettes, one hears this revelation of an artist who 'associated with God without fear'. Unintelligible to his contemporaries, they are difficult even for us. As one grows familiar with them (for all of them are now available on the gramophone) the puzzle vanishes, but only when one realizes that they are a thing never before attempted in the art of sound. This is the music of the inner life, and one compares it to Shakespeare's Sonnets. It was not written outwards for an audience, but solely, as Beethoven tells us, for himself. At first, the movements seem disconnected; an outbreak of riotous fun is followed by a cry of despair which might be a penitentiary psalm. Evidently he is conversing with himself (especially in Op. 130 and Op. 131), surveying life as he has lived it, testing his familiar theme of 'heroism', and drawing from it, but only after defiant warfare, the assurance of triumph. This was the work, not of an aged but of a deeply experienced man, subtler in technique and richer in invention than all that had gone before. His mind teemed with projects, but the neglected body was worn out. On a journey in midwinter, after a trying visit to his brother John, he caught a chill, which struck inwards and developed dropsy. The pain and loneliness of a long illness were relieved only by the generous act of the London Philharmonic Society, which sent him, as an advance, a cheque for £100. It served for his funeral. Amid a tempest, in March, 1827, Beethoven died. The life-long hymn to joy was ended as a stranger closed his eyes.

III

HECTOR BERLIOZ

By WILFRID ROOKE-LEY

FOR three days Hector Berlioz had sat, pen in hand, before a blank sheet of paper, waiting upon ideas which would not come. The paper, alas! was not ruled in staves, else had it been covered, pages and pages of it, with that musical shorthand he had had to devise, so rapid was his invention; but it was paper such as journalists use, for Berlioz had now become—and he cursed his fate for it—nothing better than a journalist. But man must live; and besides, his wife was ill, and there was little Louis, whom he adored, now six years old. . . . He has told us of those three days. 'I strode up and down, my brain on fire; I gazed at the setting sun, the neighbouring gardens, the heights of Montmartre—my thoughts a thousand miles away.'

Not really so far away as that: no farther, perhaps, than Meylan among the mountains, in the Dauphiné, and the little white house set high above the valley where Estelle lived. The name of Estelle Gauthier must stand first in any story of Berlioz. He was twelve when he first saw her; she was eighteen. It was at a party. The moment burned itself into the boy's memory: the tall girl with the large, questioning eyes, dancing upon the arm of a splendid young officer with all the glamour of the wars about him—it was the year of Waterloo, though none dreamed yet of the downfall—and himself in a corner watching them, utterly miserable. She wore little pink slippers, and the officer's spurs clanked as they danced, details he always remembered. For in that hour love was born, and jealousy; and upon the heels of love music, an overmastering urge.

He never forgot Estelle. She shone, as stars do, in twilight hours; in dreams, in the rare dawns when hope seemed rising, in dark moments of despair such as now, and in the last hours of all. ' No longer is my heaven overcast ', he is to write, years later, upon the last page of his autobiography, ' my bright star smiles upon me from afar. . . . I will think no more of Art. Stella! Stella! I can now die without bitterness or anger.'

One may guess where else his thoughts travelled as he stared at the blank paper. He was thirty-seven years of age and he had accomplished—nothing. And now he dared not dally with the symphonies that cried to be written. He was just a galley-slave, chained to this eternal drudgery of journalism. He worked it all out with the detachment of an accountant: a symphony would take three or four months to write; the parts would have to be copied—say, 1,200 francs; he would then be tempted to give a concert, and he would lose more money. He thought wistfully of pianists like Liszt, fiddlers like Paganini. How swift their victory! 'All you need', he had said to Liszt, 'is a grand piano and a large hall.' But his instrument was the orchestra—and what an orchestra, if ever his dream came true: fantastic, gigantesque, matching the tone-pictures that kept forming like fabulous sunsets in his brain. No, with a sick wife, such visions were better stifled.

His marriage had been an episode more romantic even than these visions of his art. He was a starving student at the Conservatoire when the company of English actors came to give their season of Shakespeare at the Odéon. It was three years before the revolution of '30. The youth of Paris was in a ferment; scrawling its huge red question-mark on the sacred walls of Institute and Academy; flying its new banners, and none more brazen than the name of Shakespeare. In music, as in poetry, the older values were challenged. And there sat Cherubini, at the Conservatoire, hugging his counterpoint, like Charles X his crown, as if counterpoint itself were threatened by those rascals from over the Rhine, Beethoven, Weber, and the rest. Berlioz was in the thick of it all; and Shakespeare was already the god of his idolatry. Passionately —inevitably—he fell in love with the beautiful Irish girl who played Ophelia and Juliet. But he was in the gutter; she upon the high if perilous throne of Parisian favour. Paris was calling her 'a poem, a passion, a revelation'. He wrote her letters, but she did not reply. For months he followed her about wherever she went; she invoked the police. He tried to reach her through his art—always that same cry, with Henriette Smithson then as with Paris now: 'Surely my music will speak!'; and always music meant a concert, and the infinite labours of a concert, the expense, the loss, the failure. Irony in a thousand shapes seemed to brood over his concerts, bringing his hopes to shipwreck. Yet not always, for it was at a concert, four years later—a concert that for once had been a triumph—that they met for the first time. In those four years, Paris had already forgotten her; but not so Berlioz.

Yet was it not irony in the end? Did he marry Henriette—or was it Ophelia, Juliet, Desdemona? The tinsel robes fell from her as she entered the little villa on Montmartre, leaving—what? An unhappy woman, one feels, with little brain and perhaps little charm; yet with a heart to be broken. And she was deeply in debt: she owed 12,000 francs. Hector's assets when they married were 300 francs—and these were borrowed! There was also, it seems, 'the necessity of sending money to her mother in England'; a wry note, illuminating. Manfully he shouldered the burden and plunged into journalism to discharge it. Her art had gone, and soon her health was to go and she was to grow old. And jealous. She was even more jealous of his music than of his mistress. Poor Mlle. Reccio! Another pathetic figure, of whom history tells us so little, save that she could not sing and that Berlioz was ever at his wits' end to keep her from trying. He married her when Henriette died, 'from a sense of duty'. Duty! Neither woman had much to complain of on that score. Of Henriette he would write that she was ' the harp that shared my music, my joy, my sorrows, and of which I snapped so many, many strings'. Yes; but may we not add ' for whose comfort he set himself to sacrifice so many, many dreams?' And to Mlle. Reccio he was to offer eight years' tender, patient forbearance, and when she died the tribute almost of a broken heart. Truly Irony stood sentinel over the great issues of his life. It brought him success, but never the success he craved; love, but it turned to dust. The real love-story came to him at the very end; and this perhaps was Irony's master-stroke.

At the very end, too, Paris seemed—but only seemed—to surrender: a formal surrender, like a woman's ' I cannot love you, but at least let us be friends!' For what use were the Legion of Honour, the fauteuil at the Academy, the belated little post at the Conservatoire? It was the heart of Paris he asked. He loved this brilliant, disdainful city with all the passion of his soul: it may be said that her applause was the only thing in life he coveted. But this wooing was never conciliatory: he never flattered her. Night after night he had made himself notorious in the pit of the opera, the centre of a little knot of firebrands, his red hair a sort of beacon in the dark, avenging (he would have said) the slaughter of masterpieces, by comments far from whispered; a hero to the few, but doing himself no good with the professors and functionaries—the people who counted; and on the morrow, perhaps, tramping Paris to beat up singers and players for some concert that should bring Paris to his feet. Always one pictures him in those days standing up to Paris—as he had stood up to his father over his career—firm in his intuitions, scorn trembling ever so little upon his lips, tears it may be not very far, stammering, impotent—but right!

For he was always right. We from this vantage of time know how right he was. In his writings —that galley-oar journalism—he packed all the scorn and anger of those opera-nights: the sheer sense, too, of a man whose claim to be 'the greatest musical critic who ever lived'[1] is overshadowed only by his claim as a composer. He lashes a city in which Mozart and Weber could be made palatable only by re-writing them—imagine *Die Zaüberflöte* and *Der Freischütz* mutilated for the boulevards into *Les Mystères d'Isis* and *Robin des Bois*; in which Glück and Beethoven had to be 'corrected' and re-scored; and with delicate, deadly rapier-wit he pinks the charlatan, the pedant, the pandering impresario, conductors like Habeneck, critics like Fetis. But one did not make friends that way.

'Surely my music will speak!' If it will not in Paris, it may elsewhere: and then surely Paris will listen! He had planned this oblique attack for years. Let us pause to pay honour to the man whose generosity brought its fulfilment within sight: Paganini. One day in 1838 an envelope was brought to him containing a gift from Paganini of 20,000 francs. In 1840 the Government commissioned a *Symphonie Funèbre*, which brought him a further 10,000 francs. The campaign was now possible: and it was in truth a campaign!

[1] Mr Ernest Newman.

A M. Bernard spoke once of 'Berlioz's hands that have so often led the armies of music to victory'. The military metaphor is just. He gathered his armies—those dishonoured scores that lay so idle upon his shelves: the *Symphonie Fantastique, Romeo et Juliette, Harold en Italie, Benvenuto Cellini,* the *Requiem*—and crossed the frontier. From Cologne to Berlin, Stüttgart, Hamburg, it was a triumphal progress; the march of a conqueror; napoleonic. And ever, like Napoleon's, his thoughts were on the capital: 'Another Victory! Let them know it in Paris!' ran the burden of his despatches. Almost he might have dictated them, like Napoleon, from the palaces of the conquered, for rulers received him wherever he came. Later campaigns followed—in Austria, in Russia, in England—and always amid the applause of audiences, of orchestras, of composers, of sovereigns, his ear was straining to catch the one sound he hungered to hear: the echo of that applause in Paris. But what were the laurels that awaited the conqueror at home? Those barren decorations, and the ancient apathy that was now to receive his *Faust* in silence and to drive *Les Troyens*, his masterpiece, off the stage after a few nights' run.

'I am nearly sixty-one; past hope, past visions, past high thoughts; my son is far away; I am alone; my scorn for the dishonesty and imbecility of men, my hatred of their insane malignity are at their height; and every day I say again to Death: "When thou wilt!" Why does he tarry?' These words of his herald the last phase. 'How *can* you keep any illusions about music in France?' he writes to a friend, 'Everything is dead except stupidity'. Nevertheless, he clung to his illusions —at least to one. ' I am a weary soul clutching at the past, fighting despairingly to retain the flying present. Always this useless struggle against time, always this wild desire to realize the impossible, always this frantic thirst for perfect love.' Autumn plays havoc with men in that mood, and the autumn of 1864 found him upon the hill-slopes of Meylan climbing a familiar path that led to the little white house set high above the valley. He was indeed clutching at the past! An elderly woman—a stranger—opened the door to him. She followed in bewilderment the old gentleman who wandered from room to room, and who in one room paused so long and seemed so hungrily to devour with his eyes each object it contained. ' Madame must not mind him . . . all was so strange . . . he had not been here for forty-nine years.' Yes, the room was the same ; the furniture even was unchanged. She saw the tears in his eyes, but could not know the vision that held them : the vision of a girl with little pink slippers and of a young lancer whose spurs clanked as they danced together. . . .

The past was now at his heels and hurried him along the last stage of this strange pilgrimage. That night he reached Lyons, and on the following morning he was ringing the bell at the house where Estelle was living. No love-sick boy ever awaited with more tremulous heart the answer to his first love-letter than Berlioz, standing in that hall, awaited the issue of the card he had sent up to her. Presently she appeared, an old lady of sixty-seven, with silver hair: a widow. She led him into her drawing-room. In shy sentences, in more eloquent silences, they fenced together, this old pair, fearing by a word misjudged, he to imperil the little he dared ask, she to suggest a hope she dared not offer. It was so little he asked: that he might write to her, that at distant intervals he might see her. This she granted him, and he was content. They never saw each other again. Some letters passed between them. In writing to her, he sheds the reticence that had so carefully shielded his heart when speaking to her. ' Think! for forty-five years I have loved you; you are my childhood's dream that has weathered all the storms of my most stormy life. It *must* be true —this love of a lifetime—could it else master me as it still does?' And later in the same letter: ' Do not take me for an eccentric, a plaything of my own imagination; I am but a man of intense sensibility, of eternal constancy, and overwhelmingly strong affections. I loved you, I love you still, I shall always love you, although I am sixty-one, and for me the world has no more illusions.' She replied courteously, maternally (she was a grandmother!)—like a woman who would humour a coaxing child. With such children, she tells him, ' the best way is to give them pictures to look at'. She sends him, therefore, her photograph ' that by bringing home the reality of the present it may wipe out the illusion of the past'. Perhaps in that sentence, formal as a minuet, yet so gracious, so gentle, we get our portrait of the old lady. As for Berlioz, he was at peace. She knew that he loved her. That was enough.

On March 8, 1869, he died. He had been ill at Nice, but he dragged himself to Paris that he might die among the people to whose service alone he had dedicated, in vain, his genius. But 'genius', as some Frenchman said, ' is a talent of the dead'. Here is a saying after the heart of Hector Berlioz! It might well have been his own epigram ; it may surely be his epitaph—or perhaps that last sentence of the *Mémoires*, which seems to echo the final irony : ' He was dead—the atonement began '.

IV

BRAHMS

By RICHARD CHURCH

ON May 7, 1833, a second child was born to an oddly-assorted couple in a ramshackle tenement situated in the slum quarter of Hamburg. The father was a young man, of peasant stock, who had come to town with determined, but not very intelligent or lofty, musical ambitions. He earned his living as a double-bass player, mostly in cafés. His wife, seventeen years his senior, was a plain, sickly cripple, whose only asset was a pair of clear blue eyes through which shone an honest, tactful mind and a courageous spirit. The child was a little fair-haired creature, whose eyes were like those of his mother. He was Johannes Brahms, destined to become the third of that mighty trio called by Hans von Bülow ' the Three B's ' : Bach, Beethoven, Brahms, the great architects of the house of music.

The child soon showed signs of an unusual delight in music. At the age of five he discovered that he could think of pretty tunes, and with some divine power of intuition he *invented a system of his own* for putting the tunes on paper by a series of lines and dots. Such is the faculty possessed by genius, of telescoping the laborious efforts of generations of men.

The father foresaw a future for the child. He dreamed of making him a professional musician good enough to obtain a post in the Municipal Orchestra —a cherished ambition of his own. So Johannes, at seven years of age, a pale, delicate-looking child with fair complexion and a mane of flaxen hair falling to his shoulders, was taken to a music-master of some repute in the town. Destiny began early to work, seeking to protect the young growth of this rare plant. The master, named Cossel, was a true musician, and he soon found that the boy's interest was the sign of remarkable ability. He trained him for a year, and then took him to his own master, the eminent teacher and theorist Marxsen.

Father Brahms now listened to the excited nudgings of his colleagues of the café bands, and proposed to push the child on to become an infant performer on the pianoforte. Fortunately, the awe inspired by the name of Marxsen acted as an antidote, and Brahms senior consented to leave the boy in the hands of the master. In consequence, Johannes grew and worked quietly and happily, building up a foundation of technique, both as executant and theorist, which was to be a source of power and achievement throughout his life. To the end of his career he reverenced Marxsen, sending him every composition for comment and criticism, until the old man's death at a great age. We see that the child had a narrow escape from being trained for the musical circus, to perform the usual tricks of the infant prodigy who should gradually degenerate into the flashy second-rate virtuoso, the fate of so many.

At the age of twelve he had to put a hand to the oar, in order to help to pay for his keep and his studies. He began to play in the cafés in the evenings. All day he practised, except when he was reading—another activity which showed an early development. By this time great advance had been made. Marxsen records that ' One day I gave him a composition of Weber's, going carefully through it with him. At the following lesson he played it to me so blamelessly and so exactly as I wished that I praised him. " I have also practised it in another way ", he said, and *played me the right-hand part with the left hand.*'

That story is worth preserving because it is significant of the whole man, and the trend of his development. There was always a tendency in Brahms to be concerned with technical conjuring, vast achievements of superhuman skill in the realm of musical architectonics, by which he expanded the existing rules of music *without breaking them*. The marvellous use of the passacaglia in the finale of the Fourth Symphony is a case in point. This faculty, this pride in conservatism, was what upset the rival school of Liszt and Wagner, the rebels and innovators, which flourished at Weimar. But because Brahms belonged to no ' set '—for his exploits also outraged, from another point of view, the Mendelssohnian classicists of the Leipzig school—he must not be sneered at, as Mr Shaw has been inclined to do, by calling him a composer ' whose absolute musical endowment was as extraordinary as his thought was commonplace'. I saw this idea perpetrated recently in an article in *The Listener* by Mr J. W. N. Sullivan. When we think of the incredible delicacy and variety of emotional content of Brahms' music—such things, for instance, as the slow movement in the Clarinet Quintette, written in old age when the man might be expected to have lost the power of response and sensitive observation —then we feel that it is beside the mark to condemn him as a ' second-rate ' thinker.

In his music, at least, he was *intrinsically* original ; minute and instinctive ; creating a universe of his own which, by the miracle of his conservative genius, was recognizable as a world that would have been acceptable to his great forerunners. Mr Shaw wrote his strictures more than thirty years ago, when the smoke of the civil war in musical Germany had drifted across Europe. Mr Shaw perhaps spoke then in the heat of battle.

But I digress, and our young genius is waiting to grow up. The earnest little musician overworked, and his health suffered, so he was sent for his first long holiday in the country to Winsen. Here he spent the summer of his fourteenth year. By this time he was noticed because of his ability and his striking appearance : the soft, fair hair flowing back from the broad, high forehead ; the blue eyes, intense and close-gazing, somewhat dogged perhaps ; the high-pitched voice, which never properly broke and made him very self-conscious and reticent in speech. His hostess tended him with care, sending him off for the day into the fields, a satchel of food, books, and exercise paper over his shoulder, and on his back a dummy practice-keyboard.

On this last he worked so hard that he returned to Marxsen still more proficient as an executant. By the time he was twenty he had built up a technique which astonished the great masters of the day, even such as Schumann and Liszt. Like most composers, he was at times inclined to be heavy, but there was a comprehensiveness, a mass-formation, about his playing, so that he seemed to *build up* the music afresh, giving each composition a grandeur and simplicity of structure as though it were coming direct from the mind of its composer. As an interpreter of Bach and Beethoven he seemed to make the piano sound like an organ and an orchestra respectively, showing thus the musical fundamental on which each of these masters worked. Much later in his life, Hans von Bülow—one of the Weimar school—wrote of him, ' The imagination of Bach seems, in his clavier works, to be dominated by the organ, that of Beethoven by the orchestra, *that of Brahms by both*.'

We see that very early Brahms had realized in his interpretative practice this distinction of method, and it is safe to say that from the beginning of his ambitious career he set himself to unite the two worlds of these masters into a realm of his own. He never lost consciousness of this purpose, and there is no record of an artist who so organized his life to one end. He economized in everything else. The wild oats of youth, the excitement of love, the substantiality of marriage, the comfort of money and fame ; he renounced these, and schooled himself—without much effort, perhaps, since he followed his temperament—to the one colossal full-time activity. He was a dutiful son, a great friend, and several times *almost* a lover; but these forces were always subordinated. The smaller activities and amenities of life withered in the austerity of his single passion. Being utterly devoted to his art, he gradually ceased to understand any compromise with the everyday world or with the varieties and frailties of human nature. As an instance of this, he called one day on a friend, intending to take him to hear a wonderful singer. The friend was in bed ill, and pleaded a high temperature. ' Bah ! you are a philistine ! ' exclaimed the angry Brahms, and stalked out of the house. Such conduct created a sense of solitude which surrounded him even in his most social moments. He always kept himself aloof, afraid of having time and mood stolen from him. He would never take on the responsibility of a personal home, and spent his life in furnished lodgings ! But with this aloofness he possessed a strong sense of duty and sympathy when necessity called. He loyally gave himself and his possessions to his parents and friends.

At the age of twenty opportunity came for him to spread his wings. A popular Hungarian violinist, named Remenyi—rather an emotional showman—visited Hamburg, and gave a recital. Brahms accompanied him so well that he invited the youth to go with him to other towns in North Germany. At a place called Celle the artists were to perform Beethoven's famous *Kreutzer Sonata*. The piano in the concert hall was a half-tone too low. Brahms, without any fuss, *transposed the sonata* half a tone to suit Remenyi! Only one person in the audience realized what this meant; what command of technique, what grasp of theory, what sense of creativeness. That person was Joachim, three years older than Brahms, but already world-famous, a great violinist and a great musician. Thus began a friendship which lasted until Brahms' death more than forty years later.

Joachim saw the personality that was struggling to free itself in the soul of this young provincial. He looked at his compositions, and from that day espoused himself to the cause of furthering the development and fame of Brahms' work. He began this by taking the composer to Weimar, and subsequently to Dusseldorf, where Schumann reigned as the master of the Romantics, loved and accepted by both Leipzig and Weimar; being, in addition, the greatest music critic in Europe.

Brahms was awkward and too shy to play when taken to see Liszt, who received him amid a gathering of brilliant young musicians, all prepared to be sceptical of any newcomer. Liszt thereupon took up the MSS. which Brahms had put on a side-table, and *at sight* played the *Scherzo in E Flat Minor* so well that Brahms was delighted.

It is a very difficult piece, as readers will acknowledge when they hear it some time or other over the radio. Liszt then played a sonata of his own, and the youngster was so obviously bored that Liszt was offended. Brahms always refused to temper the wind to the shorn lamb, and thus made many enemies. On this occasion he definitely estranged the Weimar party.

To make up for this, however, he found a champion in Schumann; so much so that he was almost swamped. Schumann and his pianist-wife Clara accepted the shy young composer without reserve, and Schumann, generous as usual, wrote in the *Neue Zeitschrift für Musik* the article—now famous as a prophecy—in which he acclaimed Brahms as the great one destined to come ' like Minerva fully armed from the head of Jove'.

The boy was dismayed, for he was sensible enough to realize that such a proclamation from so influential a master would mean a scathing fire of criticism on everything he might produce. His fears proved to be well founded, and for many years he had to fight against the scepticism aroused by these great expectations.

He benefited only for one year from this friendship, for in 1854 Schumann was suddenly attacked by softening of the brain, and died two years later, leaving a widow with seven children to support. Brahms and Joachim came to her assistance like sons. Brahms lived in the house, and looked after the children while she was touring Germany, giving recitals in the effort to support them. Her fame spread and with it that of her husband, to whose work she devoted her life. Brahms, too, found her a noble ally, for at every concert she played something of his, so that his name gradually became associated with those of Bach, Beethoven, and Schumann. Joachim also was working for him, performing his chamber music at every opportunity. Meanwhile he lived in retirement, perfecting his art of composition, particularly that of contrapuntal and part-writing. These activities and this propaganda, with constant output of new work of increasing power and maturity, resulted in his reputation spreading, so that by the time he was twenty-seven even sophisticated Vienna—the artist's Mecca—was interested.

In addition to this he had been accepted by Berlioz, the greatest master of symphony since Beethoven. To my mind, that was the proudest thing of all.

Henceforth, until his death in 1897, he made Vienna his headquarters, gradually establishing himself in the musical life of the city, his fame as pianist, conductor, and composer gradually becoming world-wide. At the age of thirty-four he finally established himself and fulfilled Schumann's prophecy, with his *German Requiem*. The title is deceptive, for there is nothing ritualistic about this choral tone-poem. It is rather the perfect expression of his stoic and tragic temperament: the struggle of a solitary spirit to ward off the confronting terror of death. He finds his weapon in the strength of love, that force which he was always hymning.

There still remained one field to conquer, and that the most exalted. He had yet to write a symphony. His friends and disciples had urged him, but he hesitated, for pride told him that his reputation would rest on this achievement. Not until he was forty-two did he produce the *First*

Symphony in C Minor. It was immediately acclaimed, and Bülow nicknamed it ' Beethoven's Tenth '. The other three followed quickly.

The true Brahms lover, however, finds the essence of this man's poetic genius—strange, aloof, often madly fantastic—in his chamber music. There he is found transcending all the stiffness and shy pomposity of his outward self, dancing in the light of joy, and emanating a heliacal wisdom which breaks through the classical body of his musical form like the ancient mockery that lurks in the eyes of a gipsy.

V

CHOPIN

By WINIFRED HOLTBY

IN the autumn of 1924 the patriotic Poles bore back the body of their national novelist and Nobel prize-winner Sienkiewicz from its temporary resting place in Switzerland to its tomb in Poland; at different stages of its journey, the flag-draped coffin was set down in the Polish Embassies while, as salutation and farewell, a young Polish pianist played the funeral march of Chopin. 'Chopin's music', cried one Pole to me, as I stood there in the windy autumnal streets of Vienna, 'that is the soul of Poland'. The remark has been made before. The wild, melancholy romanticism, the fierce passion and sudden gaiety of Chopin's art, are vehemently national—with the nationalism of an oppressed people in revolt, the nationalism of Poland in the 1830's. His music bears marks of the sublimated emotion of the young composer, who, in 1831, while staying at Stuttgart, heard of the capture of Warsaw by the Russians, and poured forth first in his diary, then in the '*Revolutionary*' *C Minor Etude*, the anguish of immunity. 'My poor father! My dearest ones! Perhaps they hunger? Perhaps my sisters have fallen victims to the fury of the Muscovite soldiers? And I here unoccupied! And I am here with empty hands! Sometimes I groan, suffer, and despair at the piano. O God, move the earth, that it may swallow the humanity of this century! May the most cruel torture fall upon the French that they did not come to our aid.' But it was characteristic of Chopin that he did not rush back to his family in Warsaw. He went on his way instead to Paris, and the cruel fortune fell there on his own head.

It was right that his music should be played in exile over an exile's body. Chopin's life is that of the spiritual exile. He mourned for his country, but his grief inspired not action, but music. Music for him was not the food of love; but love, patriotism, religion, adventure, and action became the food of music; he devoured experience with a poet's cannibalism, and living aloof from the country which he loved, expressed his romantic devotion in the language which he best understood. His exile was temperamental, not political. When at the age of twenty-two he found himself ' passing through Paris ', he could, if he would, have found his way back to Poland. He never did. The other element in his art, the delicate lyricism, the aristocratic fastidiousness, came from the life of his adopted city. If Chopin was a Pole by birth and passion, he was by taste, and partly at least by origin, a Frenchman and a Parisian. He belonged to mid-nineteenth century Paris—the Paris of the Romantic Movement—of Victor Hugo, of Heine, of Chateaubriand, and Lamearis, of de Musset and Baudelaire; Mendelssohn, and Liszt; of Balzac, Dumas, and George Sand.

From the beginning, the paradox asserted itself. Chopin's family was partly French, part Polish ; his father lived at Warsaw, but taught French there ; if the child Frederick heard with enchantment mazurkas, polonaises and peasant folk-songs, he played them in the salons of a society as superficially elegant as that of Paris. While only eight years old he played a concerto by Gyrowetz at his first concert. Aptly, the concert was for the Polish poor ; Chopin was a constant performer for charity ; aptly, his joy was in his grand new suit. ' Well, Fred ', inquired his mother afterwards, ' what did the public like best ? ' ' Oh, Mamma, everyone was looking at my collar.' This was the Chopin who later cultivated with anxious care the whisker on the side of his cheek turned to the audience at concerts, who, even when coughing his life away in Scotland, held himself quiet to let his valet curl his hair, and who at the height of his career wrote that his cabriolet and his white gloves ate up his earnings.

Paris was the place for such a creature, and to Paris, after an education in Warsaw and a *début* in Vienna, Chopin went. Paris welcomed him. But it was a selected Paris. All his life Chopin never attracted great crowds nor won the heart of the wide public either as pianist or composer. Before crowds, he was shy. ' I am not at all fit for giving concerts ', he said to Liszt, ' the crowd intimidates me, its breath suffocates me. I feel paralyzed by its curious look.' He, who called himself a revolutionary, whose music could interpret the primitive gaiety of peasants and the ardour of political passion, loathed the mob, shrank from brutality, and was tortured by the publicity of a big concert-hall.

But if he never captured the great world, the salons were his. His delicate and perfect playing needed the atmosphere and the sympathy of intelligent appreciation. He could not force men to listen against their will, but he could charm them by exquisite control and grace. Aware of his physical fragility, he made a virtue of his limitations. Musicians who heard him play, Liszt, Schumann, and Mendelssohn, say that, in his own style, his playing was unique.

But it is all very well to spend one's earnings on white gloves and bunches of violets, on cabriolets, and valets to curl one's hair. It is all very well to be the darling of drawing-rooms, witty, affectionate, charmingly courteous and elegant; it is all very well to be at heart torn by the sorrows of one's country, haunted by old songs, old legends and dark contemporary tales of suffering, to give concerts for afflicted Poles, to welcome with open arms and extravagant generosity all Polish visitors to Paris. There must be more personal emotion in a man's life.

There was. Chopin fell in love. Heavens; how often, how violently, how fruitlessly, how charmingly he fell in love. He began young, naturally. He fell in love with his school friends in Poland, with Titus Woyciechowski and John Natuszynski. He poured out his soul—and Chopin as a schoolboy had considerable quantities of soul—to his friends in talk and letters. When away from them, he yearned for them. He kissed and wept over them. He wrote passionately to Titus: 'My dearest one. You have no idea how much I love you! If I only could prove it to you! What would I not give if I could once again embrace you!' He confided in them and in his piano his other more devastating loves. In 1829 he wrote to Titus: 'I have—perhaps to my misfortune—already found my ideal which I worship faithfully and sincerely. Six months have elapsed, and I have not yet exchanged a syllable with her of whom I dream every night.' She was Constanzia Gladkowska, a student of singing at the Warsaw Conservatorium. He never exchanged many syllables with her, but he wrote her into music. The slow movement of the *F Minor Concerto* is Constanzia. Some of the early waltzes are Constanzia. At concerts when he played in Warsaw she sang divinely, in a white dress, with roses in her hair. He tore himself away from her to visit Posen, and there fell in love with the Princess Elisa Radziwill. He fell more than half in love with the singer, Henrietta Sontag. He fell finally, inevitably, disastrously, in love with George Sand.

Theirs is one of the world's famous love stories, not because it is one of the loveliest, saddest, most perfect, tender or passionate, but because George Sand wished it to be so, and what George Sand wanted she usually found.

This short, stout, swarthy woman, with her great placid eyes that so oddly belied the tornado of her sentiment, her calm speech mocking the torrents of her prose, and her quiet manner cloaking the ardour of her temperament, met, wooed, and conquered the charming, delicate, famous, fragile pianist. She wanted him. She had him. She came, the story goes, to a *soirée* where he was playing and stood against the door staring at him. Her marriage had collapsed; her affairs with Calmatta, Sandeau, de Bourges, Delacroix, Liszt, and de Musset were over. Chopin disliked her. He shrank from the quiet, ruthless power of her temperament. But she had him. She understood men. She even understood music. She certainly understood musicians, poets, children, and invalids. Chopin, even then delicate, was all of these.

They met in 1836 or 1837. In 1837, Chopin went out to Nohant, her country home, where he found music on the terrace, and walks by moonlight, and brilliant company, and witty talk and work. Next year George Sand's young son was ill with rheumatism. She decided to take him, and Solange, her daughter, to Majorca for the winter. But Maurice was not the only invalid she tended. There in Paris was Chopin, coughing ominously, tender, loving, beloved. Why should he not also winter in Majorca?

He did. The tragic-comedy of that experiment is one of the most uncomfortable episodes in literature. Liszt wrote of it. Chopin's comic, despairing, charming letters are full of it; George Sand made a whole book about it. And, indeed, they had misfortunes enough to fill a book. Chopin was ill. He was, according to George Sand, enslaved to his habits—to his room in Paris, his doctor, his friends, and his piano. The journey out passed tolerably enough, but Majorca was terrible. There were oranges and views, and rocks and a picturesque monastery without the encumbrance of any monks, it is true. But there was not a single hotel in the town of Palma. The beds were verminous; there were scorpions in the soup. The wet season came on. The islanders accused Chopin of phthisis and refused to let him rent either house or room. Roofs leaked. Chopin coughed. The chemist could not procure the proper drugs, and, worst of all, the piano did not come. Gradually, however, George Sand's determination reduced chaos to order. She rented the monastery; she furnished the cells; she procured the piano; she nursed Chopin; she taught her children; she bullied the domestics; she set Maurice to work in the garden: she wrestled with Majorcan farmers, who put up the price of fowls and fruit because she and her household did not go to church; she wrote her own books. Neither weather, illness, sullen peasants, nor abominable roads could quench her conquering vitality.

But Chopin was not made for camping out on islands. His cough grew worse. A haemorrhage came on. After almost incredible difficulties George Sand brought him back to Marseilles and to Paris. He was better; he was back. But his health was never quite the same again.

His friends prepared his rooms in Paris. They chose him quiet black-velvet waistcoats, dark grey winter trousers, hats and wallpaper. Always there was a legion of friends about him ready to shop, scold, nurse, help, comfort. For seven years Chopin taught pupils, played at a few select recitals, composed, spent summers at Nohant, and was nursed, dominated, loved, and stimulated by George Sand. Chopin was no slight responsibility. George Sand, while their association endured, was husband, mother, wife, and protector to him. And while she had him, she did him good. They were Arcadian weeks at Nohant, delicious evenings at her house in the Square d'Orleans. She was a born hostess, erratic, but, when she wished it, almost perfect. When he felt like playing, he played. When he felt like fooling, he fooled. He was an exquisite mimic, an amusing talker. ' In Paris ', wrote George Sand of him in ' Ma Vie ', ' he visited several salons every day, or he chose at least every evening a different one as a *milieu*. He had thus by turns twenty or thirty salons to intoxicate or to charm with his presence.' Then the rupture came. All the accounts differ. Some say Chopin preferred Solange ; that George Sand preferred her caretaker's husband ; that Chopin received Solange after she had married and quarrelled with her mother. Some, that the novel ' Lucrezia Floriani ' destroyed all hope of reconciliation. One of these things, or all of them, broke the charm. They parted, and from that time Chopin's already delicate health declined.

He came to England. He played here and there at parties ; he met Thackeray, Berlioz, and Julius Benedict ; he taught ; he received a certain amount of rather restrained attention in the Press. But the audiences found his playing lovely but lacking in vitality. He did lack vitality ; he was slowly dying of consumption.

He went to Scotland. In Edinburgh he found, as usual, friends who worshipped him. There was Miss Stirling, to whom he dedicated two nocturnes and who, it was rumoured, longed to marry him; there was Dr Lyschinski, who turned his children out of their nursery to house him; there was Mr Stirling, who bored him with heavy-handed hospitality. 'I drag myself from one lord to another, from one duke to another,' he wrote from Calder House. But lords and dukes are no cure for tuberculosis. On November 19, 1848, he made his last public appearance in England or anywhere. The Lord Mayor of London gave a Grand Polish Ball and Concert at the Guildhall. Mr Lindsay Sloper remembers how as part of the entertainment Chopin played the Etudes in A flat and F Minor. 'The people, hot from dancing, who went into the room where he played, were but little in the humour to pay attention and anxious to return to their amusement. He was in the last stage of exhaustion, and the affair resulted in disappointment.'

He had done with England. He said good-bye with relief to his Scottish friends. They were 'good, but so tedious that, God have mercy on us! they have so attached themselves to me that I cannot easily get rid of them.' There were the usual injunctions to his friends to have his fires lighted and his rooms dusted.

He returned, but he did not recover. He lingered until October, 1849, sometimes hopelessly ill, sometimes a little better. He was embarrassed by lack of money; but his friends again helped him. A Russian Countess paid half the rent of his flat;

good but tedious Miss Stirling sent him 25,000 francs. Countess Delphine Potocka hastened from Nice to Paris. Princess Marcelline Czartoryska waited on him. His sister came to him from Poland. As ever, the devotion of friends who loved him more than he loved them surrounded him. But George Sand did not come. It is rumoured that she called and was not admitted. We cannot tell. The anteroom of the dying man was guarded as though it had been a king's chamber. Between three and four on the morning of October 17 he died, peacefully, as men so stricken do. He was buried, as he had chosen, in the dress suit he wore on the concert platforms and in the Salons of Paris; the pianist contrived his last gallant and fastidious gesture. But the composer's Requiem is, for all time, his own Funeral March, its stormy grief resolved into the serenity of acceptance which is the final response of all great art to life and death.

VI

HANDEL

C. HENRY WARREN

A BABYLONISH gaiety colours our picture of London during the first half of the eighteenth century. The town took a good deal of its 'tone' from the Court; and the Courts of those early Georges were mainly conspicuous for their easy virtue. There may have been, perhaps, just the faintest excuse for George the First; he was a stranger in (to him) a very strange land. His first intention was to have a good time. If London chose to take its cue from him, that was London's fault. London did so choose—and the result was not a pretty one. Nor did things change much for the better when the King was dead and George the Second came to the throne.

In such a city, then, music must sparkle—music must thrill. And if, of its own accord, it will not sparkle and thrill enough, why, then, the Continent must be ransacked to find sopranos and *castrati* who will make it thrill. And if, incidentally, those same singers can be set at one another's throats, out of jealousy, so much the better. A singer is indeed worth going to hear when, in addition to a lovely voice, she can boast a bright halo of scandal.

Strange that, in such a city, the music of *Messiah*

should have been made. Stranger still that Handel should ever have remained in such a city to make it.

Why Handel came to London in the beginning is a mystery. He was born, of a dreamy father, in the dreamy little town of Halle, in Saxony. He was educated to be, as his father had been before him, a barber-surgeon. He might have continued on, living in that rambling old house near the market-place; inheriting his father's enviable practice; a comfort to his parents all their days, and a most respected burgher of the town. . . . But a seed of divine fire dwelt in the boy.

Handel was twenty-five when he set foot on these shores. He had already known his triumphs. When he was only eleven he had set Berlin by the ears because of his marvellous playing upon the clavier and upon the organ. At twenty, he had had an opera successfully performed in Hamburg, and, incidentally, had stirred up a mares' nest among the august musicians there. A couple of years later he had gone off to Italy, no better than a travelling musician, and had remained there long enough to find himself the friend of princes and the composer of operas that, even in that musically eclectic land, had been received with highest praise. And then, his young memory already a blaze of of gala nights in Venice, he had returned home to Germany—a little weary of success, may be, and goaded by a homing instinct that could not last for long. The Elector of Hanover had made him his *kappelmeister*. It was a fine appointment; indeed, for a youth of twenty-five it was exceptionally fine. But no sooner had Handel accepted it than he begged for a leave of absence that he might go to England. What the impulse was, who knows? Perhaps he had the very best intentions of returning to the Elector's service? Anyway, best intentions or none, he set out for London, and to London, with only the briefest exceptions, he gave his services until he died.

Thus, with no introduction, clumsy in the language, Handel arrived in England in the first days of winter, 1710. Did he still remember as he walked this strange, grey city, that Italian sunshine he had so recently enjoyed, the gallant patronage of Cardinals, the flowery rituals of Naples, the fêted performances of his opera in Venice? It must have seemed a poor exchange he had made. London had less opera then even than usual; the theatres were kept empty by fear of theft in the streets —or worse; the very streets themselves were vile with garbage.

Handel, however, did not rush off home. He stayed long enough to meet Aaron Hill, who ran the Queen's Theatre in the Haymarket. He wrote an opera for him—the first notes he penned in this country. In February it was put on the stage of the Queen's; without any high hopes, let it be said, that a greater success would attend it than had attended all the other operas that had been played to empty seats in the town. *Rinaldo*, however, set everybody talking. Who was this young man who wrote music like none that had ever been heard in London before?—and could fill the theatre, in spite of the dangerous streets? Handel was introduced to everybody. Everybody wanted to meet this dark-eyed youth who had suddenly sprung into the light out of nowhere? Handel provided, in fact, a new sensation. But sensations, as this shrewd young man knew by now, are all very amusing, only they don't lead anywhere. It was pleasant enough to dine with dukes; but, nevertheless, in his heart he longed for companionship with kindred intelligences to whom music should be more than an entertainment.

At this time one of the queerest figures in all musical history was living above a stable off the Clerkenwell Road. His name was Thomas Britton. During the daytime he sold small coals; in the evening he devoted himself to music and the sciences. He had made himself an organ; and a diminutive but perfect laboratory. He began to attract attention. Soon his stuffy little room above the stable where he kept his coals was the scene, each Thursday night, of London's first concerts— if such those strange and intimate gatherings might be called. Here came all classes of people, drawn by the common bond of music. Here came Handel. All through the Spring, while the opera lasted and Handel was still the 'lion' of the season, time and time again he escaped to this consolatory place, sometimes a listener, sometimes a performer.

Meanwhile, what about his position in Hanover? What about the Elector? Handel must return to his duties. With no great heart he did return; but on'y for a year.

London had opened his eyes. It was not in his nature, anyway, to refuse the possibilities he saw there. What a profitable field it might prove to be! The dead father was speaking in the son. A certain selfishness, a certain hard determination, a certain desire for material domination. Before he was born, his father had fought all the stout burghers of Halle, single-handed and to the last penny, over a petty legal affair connected with the sale of wine. The same zeal lived on in the son. Handel would conquer London. He would use it, making it yield up its wealth for his music. Perhaps a less opportunist mind—a Bach, for instance—would have preferred to stay in Germany, content with a provincial audience; happy enough in the knowledge that the field of music itself was the only field worth conquering. Not so Handel. The fighting strain in him saw possibilities that no quiet German town could provide. And may it not have been just that same alloy in his fine metal which gave to much of his music its rather too easy level of beauty?

Anyway, to London, in the early winter of 1712, he returned. And hardly had he arrived when he fetched out his manuscript paper and started a new opera. *Rinaldo* had been composed in a fortnight; *Teseo* took him twenty days. Its success was prodigious. The town was at his feet. The Earl of Burlington gave him a suite of rooms in his palace, and Queen Anne bestowed on him a pension of £200 a year. All went merry as a marriage-bell; and then, suddenly, Queen Anne died. The Elector of Hanover, whose service Handel had so lightly spurned, was made King of England. What a predicament! Whether, as legend has so poetically insisted, it was by way of the famous *Water Music* that the composer swam back into the favour of his late master, is a doubtful matter : the fact remains, however, that the King had not been long upon the throne when the two were friends again. So Handel went on with his prolific composing ; and the Court —Madame Kielmansegge, Madame Schulenburg, and all the rest—gave him right royal favour. Everybody was delighted—for a while.

Then began the see-saw battle with the public that lasted until the day of Handel's death : at one moment to be the pride of the town, at the next a man walking alone, grumbling to himself, shut away in a world of his own.

It was the institution of the Royal Academy of Music that brought Bononcini to England—his first and most dangerous rival. It was Teuton against Latin ; genius against dilettante. And the crowd, riding at that moment on the wave of an amazing financial boom, preferred the dilettante. So the fighter in Handel rose to the occasion. Italian singing was the order of the day : very well, then he would scour Italy and bring its finest singers home to sing his songs. If, sometimes, his genius fell foul of their finicking minds, the rough-and-tumble that followed only drew the attention of the town all the more and served, how ironically, to fill the house. (Thus it was, for instance, with the celebrated Cuzzoni ; that sack of a woman, uneducated, violent of temper. She tried her tantrums on the composer. He seized her by the waist and would have thrown her out of the window had she not quickly given in. And London thought it all great fun.) For the time being, then, Handel's star was once more in the ascendant. Cuzzoni sang his music into fame. ' Damme,' cried a voice from the gallery ; ' the woman has a nest of nightingales in her belly.'

But neither Cuzzoni, nor the adored Senesino, could down Bononcini for long. He ran a campaign against the German composer. Nor were matters helped when Handel himself added to the confusion by bringing a rival to Cuzzoni into the country. The coming of Faustina divided the town into two camps. Battles were fought in the theatre over the favourites. Racehorses were named after them. The two women themselves fought like cats upon the stage. And, meanwhile, the music of Handel was forgotten. For at that juncture *The Beggar's Opera* was put upon the stage in Lincoln's Inn Fields and the flippant-hearted city seemed at last to have found the kind of amusement it sought.

Adversity, however, only goaded Handel into fresh effort. If he could not please the fickle town, he could at least please his friends : so he retired from public life and wrote as he wished. The first result was a short religious masque. Surprisingly, it was appreciated. There was a move to put it on the stage. ' Never,' said the Bishop of London. Whereupon Handel had more words added to it, turned its six scenes into one long act, and called it *Esther*. Without scenery, or costume, or action it was ' played ' in May, 1732. The King attended. It was a success. And so was born the first oratorio.

From then, until 1742, the story of Handel's life is a pitiable decline from prosperity and public approval. He was in his forties. He had been so long in England that now, for good or bad, it was home. His old mother, who had never understood him, and whom of recent years he had hardly seen, was dead. No other woman had taken her place in his life. The thought of marriage seems never to have entered his head : indeed, it is doubtful if he understood any woman but his mother. He was a lonely, and perhaps a disappointed, man. He was in debt. He was ill. But suffering, though it may cramp the body, sometimes quickens the spirit. So, with astonishing speed, new music flowed from his pen—oratorio after oratorio—*Athelia, Alexander's Feast, Saul, Israel in Egypt.* Handel might be dead to the world, but to himself he lived as he had hardly ever lived before. Out of the sorry desolation of all his schemes the *Messiah* was born. London had refused the genius that came to live in its midst : to London's discredit be it recorded, then, that the *Messiah* was given its first performance in Dublin.

With that immortal work, life, for Handel, touched its peak. Was ever the peak of a man's life more richly crowned with stars ? For nearly two hundred years, now, that music has shed its light on the Christian story—and who shall measure the beauty it has stirred ? ' I did think ', Handel is supposed to have said, ' that I saw all Heaven before me, and the great God Himself.' And for once we need not wince lest the legend be untrue.

Not by virtue of the *Messiah*, however, did the composer climb back into slow prosperity. London would have none of it. Such music, and such a story, sorted ill with its mood just then. But if all Handel's labour brought him little money, his needs grew less and less with the years. His State pension sufficed his simple way of living. All the same, one wonders what were his thoughts of London those days. If they were bitter, he kept them to himself. And the few understanding friends who stood by him were, perhaps, all he asked. He lived, still, for his music. He wrote *Solomon* in a month, and *Susanna* in another month. His brain teemed with music. If only the body would not fail him, how much he still might do!

Once, in these quiet years, his name blazed a moment before the public eye. The Peace of Aix-la-Chapelle, so the King ordained, must be fitly celebrated. In the Green Park such a fête should be arranged as England had never seen. Buildings were erected; a huge bas-relief of the King was set up; cannon should fire a salute; a gigantic display of fireworks was planned; and Handel was bidden to compose special music. The crowds poured into the park, eager, excited. The fireworks were lighted . . . they fizzled and went out. The great building was set on fire . . . and the crowd broke into a wild stampede. Only one thing saved the event from complete ignominy: Handel's lovely *Firework Music*. The King saw what was owing to the composer. He should be properly rewarded.

But of what use, then, were those rewards—or any other? Handel was nearing his end. He kept his room—save for an occasional titanic effort at conducting his own works. The people in the park missed his strange, shambling figure;

he no longer walked there alone, muttering unintelligible words. He wrote little; and when he did compel himself to write, he had to fix his failing eyes close down to the paper. His body, that had never had its proper care, grew more and more unable. A new gentleness descended upon him. By the time 1759 was approaching Easter, Handel lay on his bed in full knowledge that the end was not far away. His work was done, the fighter in him already dead. As he looked back over the years, was he satisfied, one wonders, with what he saw? That sprawling city outside his room, did he bear it any grudge? Or was it to Halle, across the water, that his tired thoughts fled? And did he remember how, once, the great Bach, whom he so much admired, had walked all the way from Leipzig to visit him, only to find him already gone? And did he see therein, perhaps, some sort of allegory of his own music?

VII

HAYDN

By WILFRID ROOKE-LEY

THE corner of Europe where Josef Haydn was born is music-haunted. The western edge of Hungary if you examine it on a map, is peppered with outlandish names which tell of Slavonic migrations and the settlement among its rich pastures of that most musical of peoples. These names conjure up a world of romance: old castles crowning vine-clad hills, the clash and glitter of Turkish wars, the pageantry of feudalism; bands of wandering violins, the wild rhythm of their dances, the strange and lingering cadences of their melodies. Here the peasant lives his life to music; harvest and vintage, birth and wedding and burial have minted him a treasury of song. Often the Slavonic names have been softened into German equivalents. Thus Rohrau in lower Austria, where Haydn was born, is a translation of the unpronounceable Trstnik; and Haydn itself is only a derivation from a Slavonic Hajden or Hajdin. Not so very far from Rohrau is Rustnik, where Liszt was born; but the whole region is dotted with the birthplaces of musicians.

The Slav in Haydn, like the peasant, is clear in his face. The portraits are not prepossessing.

You see the high cheek-bones, the vigorous nose, which later in life became disfigured, the protruding under-lip; the whole heavy, even dour. We know that his skin was so dark that they called him 'the Moor', and that it was pitted with the small-pox. His body was ill-proportioned, but strong and wiry, like a peasant's. It amused him always to acknowledge his ugliness. But the portraits give no hint of the eyes. These were grey and large, and in them lay humour and tenderness; through them we see the soul, and that quality, luminous in his music, serenity. He had the peasant's faith, his endurance, his unfailing good-humour; and he lived to a peasant's old age. The peace of nature that enfolded his childhood, the clean orderliness of his home, a tradition of faith that was the air he breathed, bred in him a simplicity that never deserted him and pieties from which he never swerved. Never in his life was he fashionably dressed; but there was a pathetic neatness about his clothes that overrode fashion. And in his work, too, there was a method, that would have become a merchant. These things, he said, he owed to his mother.

To his parents he owed the beginnings of his music. The whole household was musical, though not more so perhaps than any other peasant household in that countryside. The father was a wheelwright. It seems to have been a family trade, for his six brothers were wheelwrights, and his wife's maiden name, Koller, was a German variant of the Slavonic *Kolar*, a wheelwright. Josef, who was born in 1732, was the second of twelve children. Two of his brothers later became musicians, but Josef's quick ear to the part-singing, his absorption in the playing of the violin by the village schoolmaster, marked him for music even in infancy. A peasant's ambition for his children is deep and romantic. There would be the priesthood, which the mother perhaps would place first in her heart; or school-teaching, for a boy who was always at his books; but here lay talent that might lead to the ultimate goal of musicianship. Suppose the child were to be one day a kapellmeister! Relatives were consulted, wires were pulled, and Josef found himself at the age of eight a choirboy at the Cathedral of St. Stephen in Vienna.

It took him twenty years to become a kapellmeister. All the adventure of his life is crowded into those twenty years. He was kicked out of the choir school at the age of eighteen and found himself penniless in the streets of Vienna. There was the adventure of starving: picking up at some desperate hour a few thalers for fiddling at a dance; or a few lessons given for a trifle. There was the adventure of getting hold of books and music; the long winter months in an attic at a cracked spinet, or pouring over the scores of Emanuel Bach, procured Heaven knows how; and the adventure of getting lessons. The renowned Porpora taught him for a time—at the charge of blacking his shoes and brushing his clothes. And there was the greater adventure of friendship: timely Samaritans finding him, when all seemed lost, a bed and food—and perhaps pupils. And there was the honest tradesman, one Buchholz, who at a crisis of destitution lent him unconditionally one hundred and fifty thalers, out of sheer Christian charity, and because he believed in him! But for the obscure Buchholz, we may ask, might not Haydn have perished; would Mozart have found a master for the string quartet, or Beethoven an orchestra ready to his hand? Perhaps Herr Buchholz saved modern music! His loan, however, was the turning of the tide. It gave Haydn breathing space. He had leisure to write; the rumour of his powers passed from mouth to mouth; and ultimately came the longed-for kapellmeistership, first with a Count Morzin, and later with no less a nobleman than Prince Esterhazy. He was now twenty-eight years of age.

The wealth of the Esterhazys was beyond compute. Their position had no parallel in Europe. The constant menace of the Turks to Western civilization, had bred this race of warriors, whose prowess in the field had ennobled them, had won them territories that were little short of kingdoms. When their menace lifted, their energy and pride turned to building. It was the dream of Prince Nicolas Esterhazy that his new palace at Esterhaz should be a second Versailles. There should be the long avenues and the groves, the pleasure gardens with their statues, and fountains, and waterfalls. The palace itself should be a temple reared for the enthronement of beauty. There should be great halls with frescoed roofs, splendid with rows of chandeliers, columned with marble;

galleries rich with the plunder of Moslem camps and the purchased treasure of Italy; a ballroom for a thousand guests; a music-room; a theatre; an opera-house; and in the park, walled like a grotto with sparkling stones and shells, a marionette theatre. The theatre should be furnished with every device of scenery and wealth of costume. The music should be the best in Europe. There should be a performance in the theatre every day; an opera twice a week. Life should be lived exquisitely to music: on the terrace, at dawn, when the Prince's hunt paraded; during the day, at some charming moment of the park, where the Prince and his party were taking their pleasure, or cunningly accompanying, like a wandering minstrelsy, some exalted guest in his tour of fairyland; in the evening, in the music-room, amid the glitter of candles and the sparkle of diamonds and brocade; and on warm summer nights, when the hedges stood out against a violet sky, music should lend its lustre to the jewellery of the stars and of the fireworks. Such was the dream; and like a dream it has faded away. Alone the music remains.

If patronage died at Esterhaz, it died in a blaze of splendour. The prince was the ideal patron. Between him and his kapellmeister there was complete sympathy. There was an excellent little band of instrumentalists and singers; and Haydn was given that freedom which is breath of life to the artist, the freedom to experiment. To modern ears, when the music of Haydn is played, it is as though a wind had blown over fields of asphodel, vintaging whatever is sweet in the memory.] It is impossible to believe that music so joyous and so simple was ever thought 'advanced'. Yet Haydn too was a pioneer; life was a voyage of discovery to him as to any supreme artist. Humour was a novel thing in music; novel, too, was the use of folk-tunes with which his music abounds. [He was the first of the 'nationalists'. And if he was also 'the founder of the modern orchestra', 'the first great master of the quartete and the symphony', this implies experiment.] How easy it is to understand the friendship between himself and Mozart! Mozart vowed he learned how to write quartetes from Haydn; Haydn's later orchestration was the inspiration of Mozart. They saw all too little of each other. Mozart never came to Esterhaz; the prince visited Vienna as rarely as he was able. Was not Esterhaz, rather than Vienna, the capital of the arts? Exile as it was for Haydn, it carried its opportunities. 'My prince was always satisfied', he said. 'I could make experiments. I could be as bold as I pleased. I was cut off from the world; there was no one to confuse or torment me, and I was forced to become original.'

Haydn was 'cut off from the world' for thirty years. Yet the little world of Esterhaz was as bustling almost and as complex as the capital. The palace and park, the country for leagues around, swarmed with officials and retainers, serfs and dependants, whose lives were ordered by strict ritual and precedent, whose bond was the service of their prince. Among them was the kapellmeister, with his office and practice-room, his position, in this hierarchy of service neatly defined, his duties scheduled and exact. The musicians had their quarters, and their liberties too were defined. Haydn wears the prince's livery with the rest, the famous livery of blue and silver; in this he has audience of his master, and presides at the harpsichord among his players. He goes to his office in the morning; he works upon the new symphonies, quartetes, operas, concertos, *divertimenti*; he rehearses. His art is not bruised, nor his soul seared. What was drollery in his music was good humour in the man; its simple themes, sweet-breathing as the country air, are but an echo of his heart's serenity. Whatever virtue carried him through those thirty years it was not tact. As soon apply wit to his melodies or epigram to his counterpoint. These are urban things; his qualities were natural. It was rather a great simplicity, a great kindliness, and the deep content of a man whose will is anchored in primitive loyalties, whose thoughts dwell in a super-terrestrial vision. He calls all men 'children'; and instinctively men call him 'father'. His musicians adore him. They too, poor fellows, were 'cut off from the world'. Their minds often enough wandered from their music to the lamp-lit avenues of Vienna. And often enough the prince forgot the promised holiday, so long overdue. They had only their 'father' to turn to; but did he not compose a little symphony in which one by one the players fade out of the score, fold their music, blow out their candles, pack up their fiddles and depart?

In comparison with so divine a joke, tact appears the blunt weapon of the bungler.

So sheltered a life was Haydn's, after the short sharp struggle of youth, that it could hardly have passed without a shadow. Perhaps it was his marriage. He had married young, at the first whisper of success, and the marriage had turned out ill. He carried in his heart the memories of his childhood; it is strange that Life should have stung him here. He was never many miles from his own people—save twice when he came to England; he spoke their rough dialect; their joys and sorrows are warp and woof of his music. We hear very little of his wife; but we know that he was a homeless man. Not in the honours that crowded upon him could he have found recompense. Long before the old prince died his name was known throughout Europe. He had received commissions from the King of Prussia, from the Grand Duke Paul, from the Cathedral of Cadiz, from Paris. And when at length the prince's death set him free, and the astute Salomon secured him for London, honours continued to crowd upon him. The audiences that filled the Hanover Square Rooms for the Salomon concerts would read how ambassadors waited upon him; how Hoppner was to paint his portrait and Oxford confer a degree; how many were the commands to Buckingham Palace. They would know nothing of the intolerable ache at his heart when the news reached him of the death of Mozart; nor would they suspect that so much adulation, so much entertainment wearied so simple a soul, and that he was often very homesick. The two visits to England were the only travel he ever made.

Vienna received his last years—those years so fruitful in mature work. London had yielded the great Salomon symphonies; in Vienna he was to write his last eight masses, his finest chamber-music, the *Creation*, and the *Seasons*. There is little to distinguish Haydn's religious from his secular music; but if he had been capable of formulating any theory he would have said simply that such labels are rubbish and that all art is religious. He did once say to Carpani that 'at the thought of God his heart leapt for joy and he could not help his music doing the same'; but the childlike gaiety of his masses has scandalized a more self-conscious age, which nevertheless delights in the gay baroque which was their setting and is to a certain extent their plastic counterpart. Unlike the nineteenth century romantics, he had no call to read or write or talk himself into any doctrine of art; the elaborate gospel of Lamennais as to the mission of the artist, which Liszt absorbed, he already lived by intuition. Was it not summed up in the 'In nomine Domini', which heads each one of his manuscripts, be it mass or minuet, and the 'Laus Deo' at the end; and is it not here, when all is said and done, that at last we touch the man behind the music?

In the Esterhaz days a Vienese writer had referred to him as 'the darling of our nation'; he was now in his old age their idol. In 1797 he composed their national anthem. Again it was a Croatian peasant tune that he took, shaped it into the fine sonorous hymn, and laid it at the feet of the Emperor, an emblem of the loyalty of his people who for centuries had borne the first shock of the Turk. Already the old order was changing. A new menace was near, this time from the West. Napoleon's cannon shattered the peace of his last days. The city had been occupied by the French in 1805, and in 1809, a few days before his death, they attacked it a second time. A shell fell close to his house. His servants were terrified. But Haydn summoning all his strength cried to them: ' Do not be afraid, children. No harm can come to you while Haydn is here.' The dying man had himself carried to his piano. His trembling fingers found the notes of his anthem and played it three times. This last act of his gathers history into a symbol: the welding of these Slavs with their Austrian masters in face of a common peril, which Time in the course of years would dissolve ; and the welding of their rustic song with the culture that came from Italy, which was Haydn's genius.

VIII

LISZT

By FRANCIS BRETTARGH

WE are so accustomed to the older portraits of Franz Liszt that we do not readily picture him in youth. There are portraits of him by Deveria, made in 1832, when he was twenty-one, and by Nancy Mérienne, a few years later. In dress he is true to period: an incarnation of the romantic movement. There is the familiar frock-coat with the velvet collar, tightly buttoned in Nancy Mérienne's drawing, in Deveria's open to show the gay waistcoat, the flowing collar and the flowing tie. But the face is more beautiful than any romantic's, than Chopin's even; not perhaps more sensitive, but more serene, more candid, and in Deveria's portrait particularly it has the radiance of innocence and an intense spirituality. He is as much a dandy as Chopin; but he has greater vitality, finer poise. Boyhood lingers in Deveria's portrait; but in Nancy Mérienne's that has all gone; humour plays faintly about the mouth and life seems already to have begun.

His early years followed closely the career of Mozart. He was born in 1811 at Raiding, in

Hungary, an obscure outpost of the vast Esterhazy estates. His father was a steward there, a man who had known Haydn, and who in that sour corner of the Empire was lonely and music-starved. Franz displayed the traditional precocities, and at the age of nine an excited father carried him off to Presbourg, where a group of equally-excited noblemen, after hearing the child play, instantly guaranteed his musical education. He was soon in Vienna, at school with Czerny and Salieri; in time to know Schubert and to be kissed by Salieri's last and greatest pupil, Beethoven. From Vienna, at the age of twelve, he was taken to Paris. In Paris he became ' le petit Lits '—le petit Mozart over again—the darling of every drawing-room, the bewilderment of all who heard him. And like ' le petit Mozart ', he went touring with his father, a meteor-like progress among the great houses and the great cities. George IV toys with his curls at Windsor; and at Manchester ' Master Liszt, now only twelve years old ' (he was actually fourteen), ' who is allowed by all who have witnessed his astonishing Talents to be the greatest performer of the present day ', played his variations upon themes ' which he respectfully requests from any member of the audience ' in the delightful conjuring-entertainment manner of the concerts of the period. Soon and abruptly the Mozartian career ends. His father dies at Boulogne; his mother hurries to Paris, and Franz, barely sixteen, must set about to support her.

It is not difficult with Deveria's beautiful portrait to picture the boy who now presented himself at the house of the Count de Saint-Cricq as musicmaster to his daughter Caroline. For it was by giving music lessons that he proposed to live. So handsome, so famous a youth had no difficulty in securing as many as he needed. But with Caroline de Saint-Cricq, the relation of music master hardly survived the first lesson. In the annals of first-love there is no story more exquisite, nor more poignant; a story that only a poet should tell, or music enshrine. One may smile to see the two children who at these lessons forgot even to open the piano; who read Dante together, and Lamartine and Victor Hugo; whose hearts, which had reached out to one another at the first glance on the first morning, drew nearer an avowal of their love, as the days went by, along the age-old path of poetry and books. One may smile at the mother, so gentle, so romantic, so sentimental if you will, who knew perfectly what was happening, and who, perhaps because she was dying, watched the children, as the dying may watch, wistfully and tenderly, some spring blossom swaying in the spring sunshine, and would not disturb them; but who nevertheless told her husband and begged that he, too, would leave them in peace. But one does not smile, or only very understandingly, at the issue. There came a day when Franz called to find the house hushed in mourning; the Countess had died suddenly in the night. No words were needed; sorrow had carried them in that hour to the last stage of their love-making, and when Caroline, white and in tears, entered the salon, in an instant their arms were about one another and their lips met. A few days later, Franz received his dismissal from the Count : a courteous, even a grateful dismissal ; and the information that a marriage had been arranged between Caroline and the Count d'Artigaux.

Such was the first love-story of Franz Liszt. It is said that it was not until the guns of the revolution of July, a year later, burst over Paris, that the boy recovered from the long apathy into which his grief had plunged him. Meanwhile, two events, pregnant with destiny, were awaiting him : a friendship with the Abbé Lamennais and his first hearing of Paganini. It was Paganini, that gaunt, unearthly figure, whose supernatural technique inspired him, first with the ambition himself to achieve even the impossible, and then with the conviction that his art, once perfected, must serve no selfish ends but must be used for the service of mankind. It was the dawn of a religion of art, which Lamennais reinforced. That Liszt perfected his art, we know ; how it was done, we know not. It seems that he received no piano lessons at all after Vienna. How he worked we never read. Perhaps it is only consonant with the splendid gesture, a sort of sublime dandyism, which it was his to exhibit to the world at all times, that the long hours of mechanical labour, day in and day out, should be hidden even from the biographer. He perfected his art ; Lamennias would teach him to perfect his soul.

But there were others : Berlioz, whose *Symphonie Fantastique* set him dreaming of the still uncharted seas of interpretive music ; and Chopin. He was soon an accredited member of that little group of romantics, George Sand, Heine, Delacroix, Hugo, Mickiewicz, and the rest. With them he plunged into an ocean of hard reading: the poets from Homer to Hugo, the philosophers from Plato to Locke, Shakespeare, Byron, Goethe. Thenceforth Byron, a well-thumbed copy, went with him everywhere; and (strange bedfellow!) the *Pensées* of Pascal. Dante, too, for Dante was to become his sovereign poet and guide. Of all that galaxy of youth, it was Chopin who was the friend: intimate, sympathetic and beloved. It was at a party one evening at Chopin's, among the flowers and the soft candle-light, and the music of his friend, that he beheld for the first time Marie d'Agoult.

When a few months later a post-chaise carried the pair of them over the frontier into Switzerland there began those wanderings that never ceased till his death. Liszt was a citizen of nowhere. Only the slenderest link bound him with Hungary; or at least his link with every country and capital was equally strong. He is now the Liszt of legend: the player whose power over audiences was superhuman, who turned the heads of all the women in Europe; the friend of kings and princes; the hero of the strangest demonstrations, the receiver of tribute and honours wherever he came; a kind of royalty himself. Those were the days of the travelling-coach, which he had fitted up like the caravan of a gipsy king, of the court of admirers who followed him from city to city, of the three hundred and sixty cravats! In England certainly he was a shade less warmly received—for the reputation of genius travelled slowly—and indeed, we read of a provincial town where he found his audience so scanty that he invited them all to his hotel, gave them an excellent supper, and then played them his programme. The true Lisztian gesture! The same gesture wherewith he took upon his shoulders the entire charges of the Beethoven monument at Bonn, to expiate France's shameful contribution of a beggarly 500 francs; the gesture wherewith in future he gave all his lessons free.

He was a veritable Midas, whose hands upon the keyboard could command the wealth of the world. It might be said, fancifully, that every note he struck turned into gold. What fortunes he made were as nothing to those that, had he cared, were his for the asking; and who shall catalogue the charity that exhausted them, leaving him at the end in the happy poverty of his beloved St Francis?

But the teaching of Lamennais soon brought to an end this career of virtuoso. His abandonment of it at the age of thirty-three, his acceptance of the post of Kapellmeister to the Grand Duke of Weimar, can only be understood in the light of the Lamennais doctrine of art, which had found so receptive a soil. Lamennais has showed him that the true aim of art is the perfecting of the creature; that the artist's vocation is to render the work of God in its sensible aspects, his highest duty ' to furnish the Divinity with modes of expression that are perpetually new '. There was no such thing as ' art for art's sake '. Liszt was thenceforth inspired with a sort of divine chivalry; his motto was *génie oblige*; and art was now first and last an apostolate which could not be satisfied by a lifetime of piano-playing. It was to be an apostolate through composition, through writing, through the championship of great music. Weimar was to become the temple of his apostolate. This irradiates many things which would otherwise be but dry facts in the record of his achievement. He had always, for instance, placed Beethoven in the forefront of his programmes; the least commercial choice that can be imagined; for Beethoven was then un-understandable, a barbarian. As with Beethoven, so later with Berlioz; so with Wagner; so with every seedling growth of the new spirit of music, the 'music of the future', as it pushed its way timorously into the untutored air of the nineteenth century; the music of Brahms, of Grieg, of the young Russian school when it arose. His own place in the hierarchy of composers the world still debates, and may continue to do so; for the issue is almost nugatory. There is no debate whatever as to the influence of his discoveries, his inventions upon every contemporary composer; nor is it fanciful to say that it is to Liszt that the world owes Wagner.

It was something deeper than the mere staging of *Tannhäuser* and *Lohengrin* at Weimar, or the mere gifts of money at moments so pressing, that one wonders whether Wagner would not have foundered without them; deeper even than the sleepless advocacy of Wagner's ideals from the authoritative pulpit which Weimar had now become; it was the giving of his soul to Wagner in a friendship so intimate, so romantic, that the world has rarely seen its like. *Génie oblige*:

and where giving was concerned, Liszt never gave ; he squandered. If shadows fell at times across that friendship, they were cast from the monstrous egotism of Wagner, between whom and a twin-deity an unclouded friendship were impossible if the other had not been caught up into the empyrean of an apostolate. But with Wagner the day came when he would publicly acknowledge his debt. It was the day of the opening of Bayreuth in 1876. All the world was there : Emperors, kings, petty sovereigns, artists, philosophers, all who could crowd into the little town, jubilant and beflagged. It was, musically, the crowning moment of the century. Liszt was there, old and venerable, an abbé now. To the vast audience Wagner said : ' There is the man who believed in me first of all . . . the one without whom you might never have heard a note of my music, my very dear friend, Franz Liszt.'

He was now the Liszt of the familiar portraits, with the face as of some old reaper who has harvested his grain and scans the empty fields that widen towards the sunset ; his eyes are filled with memories, and in the kindness of the smile there is something of satire. It is a face of infinite strength but no sternness ; the promise luminous in Deveria's portrait brought to fulfilment. Of the women who loved him and whom he loved, Caroline d'Artigaux was dead ; Marie d'Agoult, too, the mother of his children, the companion of those spring-time years when he was still the virtuoso. The Princess Carolyne was still living. For thirty years she had been the voice of Lamennais, the guardian-angel of his apostolate. This woman, dark-skinned, with Tartar eyes, a Pole, yet with the wit and the intellect of France, was a poet who could share his dreams, a philosopher, and above all a believer who could share his mysticism and nourish his vocation. The owner of vast Russian estates, which she administered herself, but which she abandoned for Liszt, she was the châtelaine also of Altenburg, the castle that crowned the hill above Weimar, which became their home. She had been married as a child, against her will, it was said, to a Russian officer, and now for fifteen years the interminable proceedings had dragged on, first with the Tsar, then with the Pope, for an annulment; and when at last the decree was about to be pronounced, the cup was snatched from their hands by a final manoeuvre of her husband's family. Liszt had arrived in Rome. Everything had been arranged for their wedding, which was to take place on the morning of his fiftieth birthday. The church of San Carlo al Corso was decorated with flowers. On the evening before they were supping together in the Princess's apartments, when towards midnight a panting messenger arrived from the Vatican with news that upon certain fresh representations from Russia, the Pope had demanded a revision of the case.

When Destiny seems cruel she is often merely symmetrical. Or she is like a musician whose modulations, intricate or harsh, can only be judged when the sought-for key is reached. Paris—Weimar—Rome. Rome was fittingly the final chord. Liszt and the Princess abandoned the struggle;

and when three years later the Princess's husband died, they did not marry. The Princess had made a cell for herself in her apartments where, with shutters closed, with countless busts of Liszt around her, amid the scent of flowers and the smoke of her cigars, and to the light of fourteen tall church candles, she gave herself up to writing; binding herself to Liszt henceforth by the stronger bonds of her renunciation and her prayers. As for Liszt, the oldest Court of Europe capitulated; it was merely the latest to do so. The Pontiff visited him in the little monastery in the Campagna, where he had taken up his quarters. The great Cardinal Hohenlohe offered him a floor of the Villa d'Este at Tivoli. There was talk of his directing the music of the Sistine Chapel, and for a time he had rooms in the Vatican itself. The soutane and the little white bands followed in due course—minor orders only, which he was free to relinquish; but a fitting symbol of the allegiance that was strongest in his soul, and a seal, perhaps, to that real priesthood of art which he had so faithfully served. Around him were the tall poplars of the Campagna and the terraced heights of Tivoli; farther, the great hills behind which rolled the country of St Francis, the valleys of Umbria, to the Tuscan plain, the country of Dante. The air was lucid like a beatific vision. To Liszt it was merely a coming home.

Yet Destiny, still in search of symmetry, decreed that he should die at Bayreuth. The old nomadic habit was strong in him till the end. One by one the links that bound him to the world were broken —Wagner died in 1883—a veritable fever of wandering possessed him. The nations were his tributaries, and like a monarch he would revisit their capitals once more before he died and receive the ancient homage. England was the last. Queen Victoria wlecomed him in the very room in which more than sixty years before George IV had toyed with his curls ; the tumultuous welcome of London is within living memory. This was in the April of 1886. In July he reached Bayreuth for the festival. He had caught a chill on the journey and was very ill. He struggled through the performance of *Tristan*, but a week later, in the arms of his daughter Cosima, and with the word ' Tristan ' upon his lips, he died.

IX

MOZART

By J. C. SQUIRE

ONE meets many people, particularly people in middle life, who prefer Mozart to any other composer. Preferences carried too far are preposterous. Leigh Hunt said: 'In the Kingdom of Poetry there are many mansions'; it is equally true of the Kingdom of Music. Different composers suit different moods; and the sensible person takes what he can get from each. At any age, men have various moods; yet with most the proportion changes as life advances. In youth a man may find an expression of himself in the turbulence (relieved by such exquisite calms) of the mature Beethoven, in the Romeo-and-Juliet yearnings of Chopin, in the sweetness and "dying falls" of Schubert, in the passionate crescendos of Wagner, the proud, wild heart of man trying to measure itself against a mysterious and illimitable universe. Later, as a rule, a reaction sets in. Those in whom there is the capacity for making music largely an intellectual pleasure tend to return to the old 'square' composers, the austere exhausters of themes whose king is the Bach of the Fugues. But others who (though they can no longer, week in and week out, find satisfaction in the abandonment of the Romantics) still crave, not only for content and consolation and the delight in perfect pattern, but for some touch of the tragic, the frustrated, the hankering, find in Mozart a composer who unites beyond all others the finest qualities of both the old and the new. No phase of emotional experience was foreign to him; yet he never strained himself and was always free from any suspicion of ' programme ' writing; no composer ever more delighted in working things out within particular set limitations, yet even the most carping could never charge him with being desiccated, or even austere. How perfectly he retained his balance on the bridge between the eighteenth and the nineteenth centuries, the age of wigs and the age of disordered hair, is illustrated by the conflicting theories of his biographers and admirers. There are those who regard him as a pure Viennese, incapable of the tragic; there are those who maintain that, if he had ever found a good, tragic librettist, he would have discovered ' music-drama ' many years before Wagner, and written it a great deal better than Wagner. There lived in Germany, until last year, a Dr Abert, who has rewritten Jahn's standard life of Mozart. This scholar wrote the article on Mozart in Cobbett's *Cyclopaedic Survey of Chamber Music*, a work produced by an amateur of genius, which will ultimately take its place beside Grove as a classic of musical history. Abert died before his article appeared: his editor found it necessary to comment as follows:

" One feature in his article will strike many readers

as a divergence from the point of view usually held by Mozart lovers, myself among the number. The composer has frequently been compared with Raphael, whose qualities of exquisite refinement and serenity of outlook he is generally supposed to possess (a nature ' profound yet limpid, all humanity with the simplicity of a child ', as Gounod said) ; but Dr Abert reads into his music qualities associated more often with Michelangelo ; tragic intensity, sullenness, even ' demonaic fury '."

Is there anyone else (excluding Shakespeare) in the whole history of human expression about whom people could argue as to whether they most resemble Raphael or Michelangelo ? And does not the fact of this controversy explain why many, when they have won through their period of ' Sturm und Drang ', find that they can listen to Mozart at any time, whereas other composers (with the possible exceptions of Bach, Handel, and Purcell) are congenial only at certain times ?

The life of Mozart is not, as lives go, particularly interesting. We do not find with him, as we find with Beethoven, Berlioz, and Wagner, that the biography throws light on the music and enriches it. He was pure composer : he ' lisped in numbers for the numbers came '. Wolfgang Amadeus Mozart (he had, by the way, a son of the same name who was a talented composer and lived into the eighteen-forties) was born at Salzburg in 1756. His father Leopold, was a violinist in the service of the local archbishop. Beethoven's father was also a menial German musician ; but the difference was that Beethoven's father, a drunken dog, exploited his prodigy of a son (thereby intensifying his fierceness), whereas Mozart's father doted on his genius of a son and proudly exhibited him. Mozart, like Pope and Cowley, is a final refutation of the easy theory that ' infant prodigies ' never develop : the truth being that they may very well develop if they are properly handled. He learned the harpsichord at three ; he composed at four ; he gave his first public performance at five. At six he toured the German courts with his father (who before long was unable to play the works that the child composed), and at Vienna won the hearts of the Emperor Francis I and the Archduchess Marie Antoinette, later Queen of France. The boy slipped on a polished floor. Marie Antoinette, marriage and the scaffold still below the horizon, picked him up. The little Mozart said to her, ' You are very kind ; when I grow up I shall marry you '. At seven he could sing, and play on the harpsichord, the organ and the violin. At eight he was living in London—first in Cecil Court, St Martin's Lane, then in Frith Street, Soho, which was also, I believe, the home of the last ambassador from the Venetian Republic. He played before King George III and Queen Charlotte. Whatever the King mentioned the child played ; he was petted and caressed, and wrote an anthem for four voices for the British Museum, which still possesses the manuscript. At ten he wrote an oratorio and astonished the Dutch by playing the organ at Haarlem, which was then the largest in the world. Then he returned to Vienna and wrote his first opera ; at thirteen his father took him to Italy.

The story is almost unbelievable. At Milan the boy was commissioned to write an opera : at Rome he heard Allegri's *Miserere*, and, returning home, set it down note for note. This prodigious musical memory was his throughout life. *Don Giovanni* was produced at Prague on October 29, 1787 ; the night before not a note of the overture had been written ; Mozart got his wife to read to him, to keep him awake, and wrote down in a night what was in his head.

Mozart fell in love with a woman—a first cousin of the composer Weber—and she would have nothing to do with him. He then married her sister. This sister was feckless and thriftless, like Mozart. When Mozart died, at thirty-five, he was buried in a pauper's grave. These two facts have led to a great deal of sentimentalism, but sentimentalism is thrown away on Mozart. It was a great pity that he should die so young ; but, dying, he would hardly bother about his grave. As for his wife, she was really just the wife that suited him. He lived for music, and she was content that he should. He kept on beginning works dedicated to her and never finished any of them ; the fact throws light on both of them ; but they were not unhappy. Mozart all his life was poor. He was one of those gay spirits to whom ten pounds seems like a fortune ; so long as the daily bread was forthcoming, large offers of salary meant very little to him. Composers, in those days, could make little money unless they obtained court posts. They were published, but then publications were sold in very small numbers ; and modern notions about copyright did not exist. There was a small salary from the Archbishop of Salzburg; there were occasional fees for producing operas to order; one way and another the wolf was kept from the door, and Mozart managed to remain in his small, dark room and compose as vast and varied an array of works as any musician of his age has ever produced.

There are all the operas—*Don Giovanni, Il Seraglio, Cosi Fan Tutti, Figaro*, with others: the total number is twenty-three—mostly seldom or never performed. There are twenty masses, including the great *Requiem*, which was left unfinished and piously completed by a friend, and which contains what he thought the best tune he ever invented. There are forty-nine symphonies, twenty-seven pianoforte concertos; there are hundreds of songs, organ sonatas, violin sonatas, quartettes, piano sonatas, and pieces composed for all sorts of strange combinations of instruments—and even strange instruments—by this man who was as curious as he was sensible. His mastery over music was complete; his emotional faculty was all-embracing. He was the greatest of all comedy-opera writers, and he might, given time and a suitable librettist, have been the greatest of all the composers of tragedy-opera. The tragic was not dominant in him. He was more Italian than German. The typical Mozart air is light and pellucid, with a touch of tenderness and a touch of sadness, northern sorrow only just impinging upon southern gaiety, yet in places—as in the tremendous entry of the statue in *Don Giovanni*—we feel that he had a great dramatic and tragic power in reserve ; and in some of the symphonies (notably the *Jupiter*) we feel that he is saying all that Beethoven has to say and saying it more reticently.

Mozart, at his best, is perfection. *Che faro* is perfection ; that song in *Don Giovanni* (which is translated as ' With a swan-like motion gliding '!) is perfection ; the Piano Sonata in A major, most completely satisfying of all variations on themes, is perfection. And it may be that the Mozart orchestra, something half-way between the domestic orchestra of the eighteenth century and the great blaring post-Wagner orchestra of our own day, was also perfection. Since Mozart, orchestras have grown and grown in size and multiplicity of instrument. More and more colour ; more and more noise ; brass let loose ; motor-horns and anvils brought in to produce something even more violent than brass. We rave, or in reaction against raving we make little, wandering noises like Debussy ; moderation, self-control, the working of ' the narrow plot of ground ' are out of fashion. The spirit of Mozart rebukes us. He knew all our ardours (not being a mere periwigged tinkler), but he knew also the necessity and the fruit of discipline. He refused nothing, but he was not carried away ; he was a gourmet not a gourmand. He had all the attractions of the Romantics and none of their defects, no incontinence ; he had all the charms of the old formalists and none of their defects, no coldness. Fashions change ; one man in each age is exalted above the others. But, in the long run, the quiet pressure of such an artist as this must tell ; and Mozart, whatever the temper of the time, will permanently stand with Virgil, whose technique is so excellent that the formalists must revere him, and whose humanity is so profound, and his sensitiveness so marked, that nobody can deny him the title of one who loved exquisitely and was acquainted with griefs.

He was the spirit of Vienna in intimate contact with the soul of all the world. He reduced all our agonies, as all our paroxysms of joy, to simple and shapely expression: resembling therein the old Chinese poets, who were blind to no fact and to whom no experience was foreign, but who felt that all life was the raw material for art, and that the soul of art was moderation.

X

MENDELSSOHN

By SACHEVERELL SITWELL

IT is an acknowledged fact that concert-halls are always ugly in themselves. Up till a few years ago their decoration, as often as not, used to rise to its climax in a series of names —they were names and nothing more—of famous composers. Queen's Hall used to be like this before it turned green, and I can remember other instances of it in the North of England. These names were spelt out in great gilt letters and sometimes they occurred at regular intervals round the ledge of the dress-circle, and sometimes they shone down from the roof.

There was something curious about those names. Beethoven was there. So were Handel, Bach, Haydn, Mozart, Liszt. Rossini and Bellini, who really were names and little more, showed near composers of whom one had never even heard mention. Pleyel, Méhul, Grétry, Spohr: these were some of them. And among them there was always Mendelssohn. But, in a sense, he was in a different category from any of the others, and there were two reasons for this. He was neglected by the good taste of twenty years ago, while he was still a popular idol with the old-fashioned public.

It is easy to explain what I mean. When I was a child you could not find a village in Yorkshire or Derbyshire where there was not an old woman who would sing you ' Oh, for the Wings of a Dove ', or ' Rest in the Lord ', if you went to see her in her cottage. The English had taken Mendelssohn to their hearts as they had no other musician except Handel.

But while he was a pleasure to many he was a pain to some few. To the cultured he meant ' Songs without Words ', the ' Bees' Wedding ' ; lots of little pieces the sound or mention of which drove one nearly mad, and a sort of general association, by analogy, with the Albert Memorial.

Now, when he has been dead some eighty years, the truth about Mendelssohn is beginning to emerge. The public have had to give him up because he was so bad for them, while the other fruits of his varied and prolific genius are being brought back again into their rightful position. Not that they have ever been forgotten, but simply that persons who despise and will not listen to his music are denying themselves many delightful experiences. The secret of this charm lies in his personality. This was formed from fertility and genius allied to a most unusual clarity and logic, qualities seldom found except in artists of the very highest rank.

But there are other reasons for it. His family were rich and cultured Jews. He never knew money worries, and I think the safety and comfort of that are audible in his music. He was a child-prodigy. The Mendelssohns had a small orchestra to play in their dining-room on alternate Sunday mornings, and at this there was always a piece composed and conducted by little Felix, even when he was so small that he had to stand on a chair in order to be seen.

Hopes were formed of him that had hardly been allowed even to Mozart. There seemed to be nothing that Mendelssohn might not accomplish as he grew older. This is not to be wondered at when his music to the *Midsummer Night's Dream* is considered. He wrote this at the age of seventeen, and it is a beautiful and unique masterpiece unlike anything else in the world. No one who has heard a performance of this under Toscanini will ever forget it. It was written long before he had ever visited England, and it shows an instinctive understanding and appreciation of England such as it is hard to believe any person of foreign birth could have possessed. Nearly at the same time he wrote his beautiful *Octuor*. There seemed nothing, indeed, that Mendelssohn might not achieve when he showed so much promise at such an early age.

His father was anxious that he should travel and meet all the interesting personalities of his time. In this way he met all the leading musicians, Cherubini, Rossini, Spohr, Liszt, and made friends with the old Goethe. He was also sent to Italy to see the works of art, but it is related that nothing, however exciting, could distract him from spending at least some hours of each day in composition. Nor did the praise and flattery, attendant on his being a prodigy and a favourite with all, in any way impair his simplicity of character. He kept himself unspoilt and uninjured through all this. But he worked too hard. Far too much music was produced by him : in his twelfth year alone, sixty finished pieces flowed from his pen. This fertility was a permanent danger to his health, and, indeed, in a sense, it killed him.

He was formed of many things. He passed his early years in a kind of Mozartian identity. His piano-pieces have that mellifluous rapidity and grace. The Rondo Capriccioso is a sort of continuation in this Mozartian tradition, but it also shows the influence of Weber and of Hummel, the virtuoso who was taken into his house by Mozart as a pupil when he was only seven years old. In fact, a famous Rondo by Hummel affords the closest comparison with that of Mendelssohn. All the formulae for this kind of music were already invented and had long been in use. They cannot have given Mendelssohn much trouble.

In this respect he only continued and did not enlarge the art. But it is a different thing with his orchestral works. In them, he was a pioneer searching after new effects, following, perhaps, a little farther along the directions that Weber had started. In his overture, *Preciosa*, Weber had made use of Spanish tunes for the first time in serious music, and Mendelssohn did the same thing in *Ruy Blas*. Landscape-painting was being brought into music with its incidents of costume and local colour. Where Mendelssohn is concerned this was more especially the case in his Italian symphony. The last movement is a Saltarello, a kind of tarantella such as was used by Berlioz in his *Roman Carnival*. This ended the symphony in vigorous and exciting fashion and was much loved by an audience who were growing accustomed to the military trumpets or hunting-horns used, now and again, by Haydn and Mozart for their finales, and to the Polonaise of which Weber made frequent use.

Mendelssohn's association with the history of taste is an interesting study in itself. Of even more importance in this direction than the Italian symphony are his pieces of music inspired by Scotland. Because of Sir Walter Scott's poems and novels Scotland had become a land of romance. It even took away a little at that time from the halo that has always been round Spain. Everyone had read Scott's novels and felt the mountains and mists of the North to be full of inspiration. And there was Ossian to be read as well as Sir Walter Scott. Even so massive and serious a mind as Beethoven's was drawn aside a little into this bypass, and the reminders of his interest in it are the schottisches, certainly the most delightful trifles left by him. *The Scottish Symphony* and the *Hebrides Overture* were Mendelssohn's contribution. They are two of his better works and they did much to increase his popularity in England.

He was a favourite figure with the British public —from Queen Victoria and Prince Albert, for whom he often played, down to remote clergymen in country parishes who had heard some hymn or anthem of his sung in their cathedral town. Had he lived, it is probable that he would have settled in England. His approach to the public was through oratorio, and *Elijah*, immediately on production, was as popular in England as the *Messiah*. It looked as if great days had come again. Mendelssohn was to become the Handel of the age, and it is interesting to think that had Handel died, as did Mendelssohn, at the age of thirty-seven, there would be little to remember him by. All his early successes had been in opera, and his most famous works were not yet written. This may give an idea of what might have been produced by Mendelssohn had death spared him for another forty years. His talent fitted in as exactly as did that of Handel with the English taste. It pleased and flattered without ever trying to startle. But that Mendelssohn would also have improved taste, had he settled in this country, there can be no doubt.

There were persistent attempts made to persuade him to write an English opera. Weber had produced *Oberon* in London, some twenty years before, and Plauché, his librettist, mentions in his memoirs how he submitted various projects and drafts of subjects to Mendelssohn, who always delayed while expressing much decision and determination to set to work. The truth seems to be that Mendelssohn knew opera to be the one branch of music in which he would fail. This can have been the only reason that held him back, for no undertaking could be vast enough to drain his fertility of invention.

He must have liked the English as much as they liked him. He had, evidently, an instinctive understanding of our race. But, indeed, it is difficult to think of Mendelssohn hating anything or anybody with bitterness. His nature was too good-humoured and urbane. His very music demonstrates a decisive change in sentiment. The days of the Regency were over; Napoleon and his Marshals were no more; the last rakes of the eighteenth century were dead. It was the reign of Queen Victoria and of Louis Philippe. The home and the family circle were a change after so many wars and so many nights out. This sentiment excuses some of Mendelssohn's melodies—or it does not, according to your individual taste—but at any rate it was only a small side, a facet, of his talent.

For there has seldom been a composer with more promise, more latent achievement lying always just in front of him. The disappointment of these great expectations lay in the fact that Mendelssohn wrote always for his own day and never in advance of it. He was a close and ideal interpreter of what was wanted; it was as if the taste of the time dictated its wishes to him and ordered their shaping into music. And Mendelssohn never interfered with this; he did exactly as he was told. This failing in courage, this easy acceptance and desire to please, can be attached too easily to his Jewish origin. The faults of that are to be found in Meyerbeer; though he, again, is a great man, and it is wrong to attack him when his music is never given, while in Mendelssohn the good qualities and the genius of his race are most in evidence.

But as well as all these other things there is his malady, his consumption, to be considered. The effects of it coloured everything that he wrote, and, indeed, made him write as much as he did. He had the usual facility and speed of the consumptive artist. He had, also, their liveliness of temperament which endeared him to a most extraordinary degree with his family and his friends. He was devoted to his parents, to his sister Fanny, and to his wife ; and I think this excessive affection, as with Mozart, was a trait of youthful character left over, stabilized as it were, from the days when he was such a gifted and wonderful child.

Peaceful as was this atmosphere of affection that he lived in, and fortunate as he was in being removed from any want of money, there were, even yet, many exasperations and worries in his life. These were concerned, chiefly, in the production of his own works, and things which would not have been much nuisance to a man of tougher fibre, wore Mendelssohn down and helped to kill him. He was interested in much other music, besides his own, but chiefly and principally in the great Bach. Every lover of beauty owes Mendelssohn a debt of gratitude for his enthusiasm over this ; and, but for him, many works of the master would have been lost to the world. Mendelssohn's campaign to rescue his works and publish them came just in time ; in another few years they would have been gone irretrievably.

As he grew older his concerns, as was natural, increased in scope and in variety. They began to tell on his health, but the fatal blow from which he never recovered was the death of his loved sister, Fanny. When this was broken to him Mendelssohn fell to the ground, insensible. It must have been a kind of seizure, but when he got over the immediate effect of it he was left a hopeless and morose invalid. He had no longer any desire to write music, and in hopes to save his life his family conveyed him by slow stages to Interlaken.

There he made a recovery and his health improved slightly for some months. He only wrote a few songs and part of his last oratorio, *Christus*, said to be a work of peculiar beauty and strange character. Instead of writing music, for which he had still but little inclination, Mendelssohn spent his last few months in painting a series of large water-colour pictures of Swiss scenery. These are said to have been most successful productions of their kind, and it would be interesting to know what has become of them. It is possible that they still belong to his family in Germany. But he began to decline again, and on taking his last songs to be sung by a friend of his he had another and fatal seizure. This time he lingered for four dreadful weeks, and then died.

He was one of the most natural and fluent composers there have ever been, and the mere mention of these two characteristics makes a criticism of our own age that we live in. Convention, formula are dead now. That is why every old building, and every old piece of music puts us to shame.

Rules and principles of architecture should govern everything, and when they do the greater geniuses break them and men of less talent keep to them and produce an infinity of good work.

XI

MUSSORGSKY

By C. HENRY WARREN

THEY were called 'the Five'. Their names, were Balakireff, Borodin, Rimsky-Korsakov, Caesar Cui, and Mussorgsky. They lived (for the greater part) in the St. Petersburg of the 'sixties and the 'seventies, talking, thinking, and making music. Their watchword was Nationalism, and out of their enthusiasm grew the music of the new Russia.

The father of the little group was Balakireff, kindly, wise, and a trifle didactic. But if Balakireff was the father, Mussorgsky was the wayward child. He insisted on remaining obstinately himself. Balakireff might dictate, but Mussorgsky would never obey; Balakireff might insist on the necessity of golden rules, but Mussorgsky was for ever giving them the lie. Until his death his friends were always pointing out the right way, only to see him take the opposite direction. So when he was at last in his grave, one of them gathered up his work and re-shaped it, making it (as he sincerely believed) more acceptable to the world.

Modeste Mussorgsky was the son of a small land-owner living some four hundred miles south of St

Petersburg. He was born in 1835. The first ten years of his life were spent in rural remoteness. The country was in his blood. Until the end he retained a sympathetic understanding of the peasant that altogether astonished his urban friends. His brother once wrote of him that ' he considered the Russian moujik *a true man* '. Where others could see nothing but ignorance and sloth, Mussorgsky detected innocency and simplicity of purpose. Nor was this mere sentimentality—the wearing of rose-tinted glasses. No man ever lived more naked-eyed than Mussorgsky.

It was from this almost telepathetic understanding of the natural life that the composer drew his art. This peasant simplicity he understood : sophistication was to him a foreign tongue. He tells how, for instance, sitting one day at his window, he watched the village simpleton trying to make love to the village beauty. The boy's blushing awkwardness, as he strove to awaken the pity of the girl, seemed to speak a slow comprehension that the joy of love could never be the lot of such as he. Deeply moved, Mussorgsky set down in song the baffled soul of that Russian idiot ; and the consequent music is terrible in its harsh realism. Or again, writing to Cui from the country, he said, ' This stinking atmosphere affects my feeling for beauty in a remarkable way : one thinks exclusively of how not to be vitiated, how to avoid asphyxiation—and of how to think all this out in music.'

Circumstances compelled this country-hearted man to live a good deal in St Petersburg. At seventeen his parents had entered him in the school of the Ensigns of the Guard, and four years later he left the school to join the Preobraiensky regiment. Of the man he was one day to become there was then little, if any, apparent indication. ' We met accidentally ', said Borodin of him at this time ' in the orderly-room of the hospital, both being on duty. . . . The same evening we were invited to the house of the chief doctor. Mussorgsky was then a veritable fop, very elegant, a fine type of young officer ; his well-fitting uniform all spick and span ; his hair well brushed and pomaded ; and his hands well cared for like the hands of an aristocrat. His manners were exceedingly refined : he spoke mincingly and was lavish with his French phrases. He would sit at the piano and, with elegant gestures, play portions of *Trovatore*. The ladies were charmed with him. . . .'

Underneath the temporary fop, however, hid a rugged soul that soon was to burst its delicate husk.

In violent agony a new Russia was being born. As soon as Alexander II ascended the throne the emancipation of the serfs had begun. All looked fair for a new Russia. But a system of such revolutionary character is not inaugurated with ease, and the Czar's promises were not always followed by fulfilment. Underneath, a ferment of unrest was constantly working among the people—a moral and intellectual ferment. There were riotings from time to time. Attempts were made to assassinate the Czar. Mussorgsky must have seen loads of Nihilists driven away to their death. No artist could live in the centre of such disruption and not be profoundly moved. In the city a new cry was heard: 'Let Truth be your aim, and not Beauty.' At the old precept of Art for Art's sake they pointed a finger of fierce derision. Onwards Art must be the handmaid of Humanity. All this affected Mussorgsky to his core. His sympathy with the peasants made him feel strongly associated with their sufferings in this fierce fight for emancipation; and the revolutionary gospel of the artists made the strongest possible appeal to him—Mussorgsky, who was country-born, sensitive to the simple joy and sorrow of the peasants, imbued with an understanding of them that was deep and hurting as life itself—Mussorgsky, to whom the still sad music of humanity was the most poignantly real thing in all life.

No wonder, therefore, that he turned to music with a new earnestness. A purpose had leapt into his life. He would use music for the faithful expression of things as he saw them. To do this, he felt, he must resign from his regiment. Friends might try to prevent him, counselling him to a compromise, pointing to the example of Lermontoff, who had managed to be both soldier and poet at the same time. 'Lermontoff and I', was his quick retort, 'are very different persons. He was able to accommodate himself: I cannot.' Now that Mussorgsky had made up his mind, it was all or nothing. He resigned.

From then onwards his days were one long and bitter fight with poverty. At one time we find him translating into Russian the proceedings of great criminal cases, so that he may keep the body alive. At another time he has somehow secured a minor

Government post. And at yet another time we find him compelled to sacrifice the freedom essential to the artist for a meagre appointment in the Ministry of Woods and Forests. Rimsky-Korsakov, Balakireff, and the others might climb to fame and even to wealth on the fine wings of their music; but Mussorgsky remained the slave of poverty, almost unknown, almost unheard. He was nearly forty before he received his first tribute of flowers.

Through all this time, however, he was gradually clarifying his conception of the aim of a true artist. 'Art', he wrote, 'is a means of conversing with men, and not an end in itself.' He wrote some songs, and they were like none that had ever come out of Russia—or, for that matter, anywhere else. They were human documents. He watched the beggar in the street, and the music he made of his vision seems the very voice of that wretched man's suffering humanity. He watched the peasant-mother feeding her babe at starved breasts, and the cradle-song that flowed from his pen is like a final expression of tragic motherhood. He watched the spindle-shanked schoolmen going through life blinded by pedantry, mixing their love-making with a jabbering declension of Latin substantives, and the song he made of it is a whip of scorpions against the unwisely wise. Whatever it was that he turned into song, the same grim realism pervaded it; sometimes deeply tragic, sometimes satirically humorous, and always violently naturalistic.

These songs, like everything else he wrote, were shown to friends and critics. How little they were understood ! Of course, he was praised—the man had such obvious genius ; but if only he would pay some attention to rules ! All very fine (one can hear his critics saying), but you won't win fame on that kind of stuff. Rules, my boy, rules—there's more in them than you think. . . . But rules are not made for such as Mussorgsky, save to be broken. He was his own rule. It was of no use for the academicians to chatter away in their jargon. This was all the effect they had on him :

' Tell me why (he wrote) when I listen to young artists, painters, or sculptors talking, I can follow their thoughts and understand their aims ? I rarely hear these people talking technically. On the other hand, when I am with musicians, I seldom hear them express a single living thought. One would think they were all on school benches. They only understand " technique " and technical terms. . . .'

So we have the picture of him in St Petersburg, superficially one with the rest of the group whom circumstances labelled together with him as ' the Five '. Yet how strangely at odds he was with them underneath ! Years later, when he was dead and his musical manuscripts were handed over to Rimsky-Korsakov to prepare for publication, this is what that famous composer—master of oriental colour, and luscious harmony, and gallant rhythm—wrote in his diary : ' They were in exceedingly imperfect order ; there occurred absurd, incoherent harmonies, ugly part-writing, now strikingly illogical modulation, now depressing absence of any at all, ill-chosen instrumentation, in general a certain audacious, self-conceited dilettantism, at times moments of technical dexterity and skill, but more often of utter technical impotence.' Time brings strange revenges.

In all the coming and going, then, between the various places of meeting, the one odd figure among 'the Five' was Mussorgsky. Ill-sorted as he must have been to them, he needed their company. The artist cannot live alone. Nevertheless, he was the cuckoo in the nest. Against their charming singing, his voice sounded harsh and uncouth. Try as they might, however, they could not make him sing in any other way.

Thus the years passed, now in the midst of the first musicians in the city, now home again in the country. He carried on with his music-making: songs (like the boisterous 'Song of the Flea' or the humorous pastoral 'Gathering Mushrooms'), the opera *Khovanshchina*, and various orchestral and instrumental pieces. The others made names for themselves, their music was heard all over Europe, they were lauded at home for the bright renaissance they had brought to Russian music. But Mussorgsky was scarcely heard of, his music remained the pleasure of a very few, he seemed to have done nothing for his country in its flaming rebirth. Poverty, that romantics so glibly suppose is the right and proper portion of the genius, gradually wasted him, robbed him of his health, took away his strength, even, at last, began to undermine his lucidity of mind.

He was not to die, however, before he had given to Russia its masterpiece of music-drama, its great national opera. It was a friend who, with miraculous insight, suggested the theme of *Boris Godunoff*. A subject more congenial to the composer it is impossible to imagine. Pushkin had already given it the immortality of poetry : Mussorgsky read it and gave it the second immortality of music. The tragic tale fired his mind. It concerned one of the most dramatic incidents in all Russian history. The heir of Ivan the Terrible was weak-minded and the real power passed into the hands of a regent, the strong and crafty Boris. Had it not been for Dmitri, the younger brother of the Tsar, Boris would have climbed to kingship itself. So Dmitri was done away with. Then a Pretender came forward, a young monk who claimed to be the dead brother of the Tsar, and a dreadful Nemesis overtook the mighty regent. . . . On such a theme, working at terrific speed, Mussorgsky put a complexion of national tragedy the like of which has never been equalled in opera. He disregarded all the operatic conventions ; beyond Boris, he provided but few principal roles ; he filled the stage, continually, with great hordes of people ; and he made the work of a length calculated to scare the most enthusiastic producer. It must be changed, said the Director of the Opera House. It was changed—but even so, in 1874, when it was given its first full performance, the majority could not tell what to make of it. It was like nothing they had ever heard before : huge, terrifying, rough, flooded with mob-passion, barbed with living satire, crude.

Nevertheless, the younger generation seemed to grasp it. Groups of excited students could be heard shouting its choruses far into the night, as they swung home across the Neva, arm in arm. It roused the city to a battle royal. So tense did feeling become that when the composer's admirers wished to present him with appreciative wreaths, the infuriated critics blocked the passages to the back of the stage, so that they were obliged to take their flowers home with them and deliver them the next morning. The opera played for twenty consecutive nights—a triumph of the wildest kind. Then this Dostoievskian opera was withdrawn.

Mussorgsky's greatest work was accomplished. Nevertheless, his rapidly declining health could not completely damp the fires of inspiration : but it needed urgent cause to spur him into the active creation of music. One such spur was provided by an exhibition of water-colours, the work of a dead friend, Victor Hartmann. Mussorgsky was profoundly moved: as an act of homage he sought to reproduce some of the paintings in terms of music. Other works, attributable to this period are the opera *Khovanshchina* (which he finished), and the barely started opera *The Fair at Sorotchinsk*—of which the *Gopak* is perhaps the best-known of all his music. To this pathetic period, too, belongs the tour he made, with the singer Leonova, into the south of Russia, where a series of concerts was rewarded with considerable success—a flicker of fame before the end ; for when the composer returned from this tour it must have been apparent he had not long to live. 'Examine yourself', he once had said : 'have you claws, or only smooth stumps ? Are you a deer or a web-footed creature ? Where are you ?

Outside the barrier? . . .' But now his own claws were blunted : the deer in him was all but dead.

He had sunk back again into the shadow, poorer than ever, feebler in health, and driven at last to the morbid consolation of drugs. He gave up his government appointment. He lay about, broken and ill. He looked (as Repin's picture, painted at this time, realistically shows) a mere travesty of the man he once had been. Where was the stalwart soldier-type now ? Where was the onetime fop ?

At last he was compelled to enter a hospital, and there, on his forty-sixth birthday (1881), he died, the greatest example of natural genius that modern Europe has to show ; the completely unsophisticated artist, broken on the wheel of cruel circumstance.

XII

SCHUBERT

By J. W. N. SULLIVAN

SCHUBERT is, above all musicians, the poet of moods. Of all the really great musicians he is the most sensitive to impressions coming from without. He is for ever giving expression to something that has been aroused in his soul by an external stimulus. That is why he is essentially a lyric poet, incapable of the prolonged and logical development of the epic. Beethoven gave expression to the development of the inner life. His work reveals a profound nature of extraordinary depth and integrity, capable of an organic growth uninfluenced by what he called 'the storms of circumstance'. Mozart, although he was, later in his life, influenced by experience, was, for the most part, as independent of the teachings of life as is a mathematician. The world he created has its own laws and exists in its own right. It is not a copy of the world of experience, nor does it express the composer's reactions to it. It is as ideal as, and even more beautiful than, the world of pure mathematics. But Schubert was at the mercy of every wind that blew. A storm, the sudden vision of a field of flowers, a girl's sigh, the solemn pulse of the ocean, were events that Schubert accepted with a pure sensitivity almost unequalled, and were immediately transmuted, by his rich and delicate nature, into sound. Hence the fact that he was, from the beginning, primarily a song-writer, and that he wrote his songs in extraordinary abundance and with extraordinary rapidity.

A song expresses, for the most part, a mood. It seizes a transient emotion on the wing, as it were. A great song-writer must be, above all, rich in responses. We may say, indeed, that his emotions must be easy and fluent rather than profound. It is not his task to *explore* an emotion, a Beethoven did, to grasp it in all its complexity, to make it ever more profound. This requires a degree of profundity, and a power of development, for which the song is an altogether inadequate medium. The function of a song writer is to present an emotion in its immediacy, without pondering upon its significance. To this end the song writer must have a most delicate and responsive nature. He is likely, indeed, to be comparatively lacking in depth and ' balance '. His inner life will be extraordinarily rich and varied, but it is not likely to show a steady development. Hallucinated and absorbed as he is by the lovely and distracting surfaces of things, he is not likely to develop a philosophy of life nor to make his career as an artist a step by step progress towards some distant goal. He is likely, in fact, to seem something of a dreamer—even a drifter. The value of his work will depend on the range and acuteness of his sensibilities, and on his power to convey his impressions. Essentially he is to be regarded as a sensitive and transfiguring magic mirror. His function is to reflect life, not to understand it or to justify it.

We find in Schubert all the characteristics of the great song-writer. To his contemporaries he seemed to lack strength of character, to be incapable of a fixed purpose. His lack of material success they attributed to his laziness, his shiftlessness. They regarded his extreme sociability as almost a vice. Schubert knew nothing of loneliness. He was always surrounded by a group of friends, writers, painters, musicians. He spent much of his time in taverns, talking and hearing talk. He loved going to fresh places and meeting fresh people. He was eager, intensely alive, avid of impressions. And, indeed, these changing impressions, these varied emotions, were the food on which Schubert the artist lived. When life seemed flat he would go to a wine cellar and there spend the little money he had on drink. The drink excited him; it enabled him to dream and see visions; it made life worth living again. These characteristics are what we should expect from his music. No artist ever lived whose sensibilities were so delicate and numerous. In the hundreds of songs that Schubert has written we find expressed a really amazing variety of impressions. It seems that he could seize and body forth any mood, however elusive, however transient. His emotional nature stirred to the slightest impulse; it was, as it were, adjusted with infinite delicacy. And his work suffers, of course, from the disadvantages that attend such facility. He was incapable of the logical expansion of an idea, of the profound and unflinching development of an emotion. He was incapable of the intensity of realization, and also of the coherence, displayed in such a work as the slow movement of Beethoven's *Ninth Symphony*, for example. It is for this reason that Schubert's large scale compositions, although they contain some of his most wonderful music, do not exhibit the mastery we find in his songs. Schubert was incapable of a really sustained flight. But although Schubert could not develop a theme, in the Beethoven manner, he could always invent a fresh one. The wealth of melody to be found in his music is unequalled.

It is characteristic of the Schubert type that such artists are great only in their art. They are passive rather than active, reflective rather than forceful. As a result, they lack 'personality.' In everything outside music Schubert's ideas, like his character and appearance, were entirely undistinguished. His musings on life, as exhibited in his diaries and letters, are sentimental, romantic, imitative. He was modest, but his modesty seems to have been the result of shyness as much as of anything. It is inconceivable that a man of Schubert's genius should not have known who and what he was. But it suited his placid, passive temperament rather to have his claims ignored than to assert them. Nevertheless, there were limits to his indulgence. He would rise up in his wrath when he felt that the god in him was really being blasphemed. Bauernfeld relates that on one occasion, when the members of a famous Viennese Orchestra, in the course of a dispute with Schubert, claimed that they were as good artists as he was, Schubert shouted, 'Artists! Artists! *You* call yourselves artists! One of you bites between his teeth a wooden tube, the other blows out his cheeks playing the bugle! Do you call that art! It's just a piece of mechanical trickery that brings in pence. Fiddlers, windblowers! That's what you all are. Nothing else. But I am an artist. I! I am Schubert—Franz Schubert, whom all the world knows, who has done things that are great, beautiful; things of which you have no conception; and I shall do more beautiful things. For I am not just a mere bungling country composer, as the stupid newspapers think. Let the fools talk as they like.'

But although Schubert knew who and what he was, he also realized his shortcomings as an artist. He was a contemporary of Beethoven, and all his life was overshadowed by that mighty genius. And Schubert was particularly fitted to appreciate Beethoven. It was in virtue of his very weaknesses that Schubert, more than most, could appreciate the profundity of Beethoven's conceptions and the masterliness of his grasp. Beethoven never had a more ardent worshipper than Schubert. At the very beginning, as a mere boy, when Schubert confided to Spaun his ambition that he would one day write music, he added, 'But who dare attempt anything after Beethoven?' When he was a famous composer his consciousness of the gulf between himself and Beethoven remained. As he once explained to the author, K. J. Braun, 'Beethoven can do everything, but we cannot understand everything, and much water will be carried away by the Danube before people arrive at a complete understanding of what this man has created. Not only is he the most sublime and prolific of all composers, but he is the most courageous. He is equally strong in dramatic as in epical music, in lyrical as in the prosaic ; in short, there's nothing he cannot do.'

This feeling, admirable as it appears, was in some danger of becoming an obsession. It prevented Schubert from becoming intimate with Beethoven, an intimacy which, when he came to know Schubert's work, Beethoven would have welcomed, and which would certainly have been to the advantage of both men. And it may have hindered Schubert in manifesting that self-assertion so necessary to success. It may have induced what is called, in modern jargon, an ' inferiority complex '. It is significant, in this connection, that Schubert, on his deathbed, rejected his brother's attempts to console him with the remark, ' No, it is not Beethoven who is lying here ! '

It is customary to say that Schubert led an unhappy life, but there is no evidence that he had any profound sorrows. He was chronically hard up, for his music was sufficiently unconventional for publishers to be shy of it. He tried once or twice to get musical appointments, but had not sufficient influence to succeed. He lacked the energy and practical sense to engineer public concerts of his works. He seemed, indeed, fairly well content with private performances in the houses of his friends. He was the most unenvious of men, and almost wholly lacking in ambition of the worldly sort.

But he was ambitious as an artist; he always wanted to do better. And he worked extremely hard. His real life was in his musical imagination. For the rest he was an ordinary person who led a pretty ordinary bohemian life. He was used to poverty. His father was a schoolmaster, and Schubert himself was an assistant schoolmaster for a time. But he quite deliberately chose the chances and troubles of an insecure bohemian existence rather than endure that slavery. He was often hungry, and he was probably never free from anxiety about money. But it would be absurd to pretend that he was brought to an early death (he died at thirty-one) by the indifference or hostility of the world. He died, as a matter of fact, from eating bad fish.

It is not possible to see Schubert in his life. His amours, his relations with his friends, his talk, his letters, are all quite unrevealing. The real Schubert, the Schubert who ranks amongst the few great musical geniuses of the world, was no more apparent in his life than in his appearance. Here is a description of his appearance, that Kobald has gathered from accounts of his contemporaries: ' He was short, his face round, fat and puffy—" Schwammerl ", his friends nicknamed him. His forehead was low, his nose of the snub variety, his dark hair extremely curly, which gave him a somewhat nigger-like appearance. He always wore eye-glasses even in the night, so as to be ready to compose directly he woke in the morning. His expression was, as a whole, neither intellectual, distinguished, nor genial. Only when he was composing did his face change and become interesting, almost demoniac. Then his eyes would flash with the fire of genius. " Those who knew Schubert intimately ", writes his friend, Josef von Spaun, " saw how intensely his creations moved him, and how often they were born in pain. When one beheld him in the morning at work, with flashing eyes and glowing cheeks, another being altogether from his usual self, one received an impression not easily forgotten ". '

He was born in 1797 and died 1828.

XIII

TCHAIKOVSKY

By JOHN MANN

IN 1885 the casual visitor to Maidonovo near Klin, halfway between Moscow and St Petersburg, would have noticed that the morale of the villagers was being affected. He would observe that they disappeared on lengthy and mysterious excursions and returned, generally, with disappointment in their eyes. What were they doing? Dogging the Hermit of Klin in his solitary rambles. Popping up in front of him when he thought he was most alone, with a smirk obviously meant to prompt a tip.

Really it was the Hermit's own fault. When he had gone to live at the decaying Villa Maidonovo he had distributed largesse among the children with thoughtless generosity. The infection had spread to the parents, and now the whole village had a watching, predatory look. The inhabitants skulked outside the gates and laid ambushes about the forest walks. Casual visitors themselves, trippers from the great civic centres, did much the same thing, though with the comparatively pure motive of curiosity. For might they not catch a glimpse of Tchaikovsky, composer of an Empire's music, of whom greater and greater things were expected?

So Peter Ilich Tchaikovsky discovered that a country life is all very well when you are unknown: when you are celebrated it is merely making a silhouette of yourself. 'Alas', he writes, 'the lovely park, the beautiful views and the splendid bath, are all alike spoiled by summer visitors. I cannot take a step in the park without coming across some neighbour.' Yet the fact that the tourists were more or less right, that there was a great work on hand, was some consolation. Rather, one should say, two great works, an opera, *The Enchantress*, which was to eclipse all his previous efforts of the kind, and a programme symphony based on Byron's 'Manfred'. Presently came suffocating fogs from the near marshes, fogs which drove away unwelcome visitors and deepened the gloomy mood necessary to give atmosphere to such works.

At this time, as almost to the end of his career, by far the greater part of Tchaikovsky's correspondence was with Madame Nadejda von Meck, a widow ten years older than himself, with a fortune, a large family, and an enthusiasm for music. Eight years previously she had heard Tchaikovsky's compositions and had fallen in love with them. Too strong-minded to delude herself with dreams of an actual alliance with a young and struggling composer she had held out a richly helping hand, given him nobly extravagant payment for small compositions which she ordered, and, to crown her generosity, made him an annual allowance, disarming his scruples with the words, ' My most precious beliefs and feelings are in your keeping ; your very existence gives me so much enjoyment. So, you see, my thought for your welfare is purely egotistical, and, so long as I can satisfy this wish, I am happy and grateful to you for accepting my help.' The pair of idealizers thenceforth determined to put Romance to the severest test. As friends they never met, and when they did accidentally they treated each other like strangers. That was tacit, and perfectly understood. But in their letters they poured out their souls to one another, voiced the warmest sentiments with the artlessness inherent in the Slav nature, exchanged photographs, views on life and opinions on music with the utmost freedom and intimacy. Plato must have made approving gestures among the shades at this perfect practice of his theory. But in the end it brought tragedy to Tchaikovsky, and the great sorrow of his life when he could least bear it.

True, he had had two other affairs, but neither of them brought to him the intellectual satisfaction for which he craved, and with which Nadejda, his mother-confessor, supported him as well as with the pension. In 1868, when a Professor of Harmony at the Moscow Conservatoire and soon after the composition of his first symphony, he heard Desirée Artôt, a soprano of passing fame, plain but fascinating, sing at St Petersburg. Unlike many *prima donnas* she was a splendid actress, and Tchaikovsky found her as captivating in private life as she was on the stage. His friends, especially Nicholas Rubinstein, who saw where he was heading, did their utmost to curb him. Tchaikovsky in his trouble wrote a long and anxious letter to his father. He was not earning enough, he said, to keep them both, and if he married it might mean the end of his musical career, for his wife—so his friends said—might insist on turning him into a sort of henchman, and monopolize his time for her service. The fond and sentimental old man replied with a screed full of unhelpful, romantic platitudes. A month or two later we find Tchaikovsky saying: ' With regard to the love affair I had early in the winter . . .'—a brisk and businesslike reference indeed—after which it is not surprising to hear that he was too absorbed in an opera to be deeply hurt when he heard of her sudden marriage in Moscow to a fellow singer. Nevertheless, when he saw her on the stage shortly afterwards he kept his opera glasses glued upon her, tears streaming down his face the while. When they met again, twenty years on, no sign of their old passion remained in either. They had reached the commonplace anti-climax of mere friendliness.

Then there was his wedding, a wildly farcical affair which nearly cost Tchaikovsky his reason. It was one of those things which should never have occurred, but are probably inevitable. From start to finish the affair is staggering in its fantasy. The first we hear about it is in a letter to his brother Modeste in 1876, when he says his reflections have resulted in the firm determination to marry some one or other. This determination persisted through several letters to other correspondents, but for a time disappeared on his first making acquaintance with Nadejda. To her he wrote the letter announcing his engagement, surely the strangest in the annals of matrimony. A lady, he said, had written to him saying she loved him. He tried to reason with her—' I described to her in detail my character, my irritability, my nervous temperament, my misanthropy, finally my pecuniary situation '. Confidently Tchaikovsky put the question—and terribly, she accepted him. Terribly, for listen : ' The agonies I have endured since that evening defy description. To live thirty-seven years with an innate antipathy to matrimony, and then suddenly, by force of circumstances, to find oneself engaged to a woman with whom one is not in the least in love—it is very painful '. Her name was Antonina Ivanovna Milioukov, and she was aged 28, good looking, of spotless reputation, capable of a loyal attachment—in fact, Everywoman.

His father was delighted, the rest of the family maddened. They were justified, for Tchaikovsky, having married on principle (with a last attempt to lay the blame on Fate), was to repent in practice. As his wife prepared their home in Moscow, a nervous crisis prepared itself in Tchaikovsky, and nine weeks after the wedding it revealed itself as a condition approaching insanity. He separated from his wife—whom he was emphatic was not to blame—and was taken by his brother Anatol on a journey of recovery to Switzerland and Italy. The experience was a warning to him, and never again did he embark on an emotional exploit. Other adventures of the spirit he had, but they came to him, he did not seek them. All he wanted was a quiet country life in which he could compose *ad infinitum*. But by the time he had got a country house of his own fame had begun to show her claws. With them she dragged him, from his retirement at Klin, upon a world clamouring for him to be a conductor as well as a composer. He who, in his youth, had hated conducting so greatly that he said: ' When I stand on the platform I feel as if my head will come off ', and to prevent it happening held his chin with one hand while he waved the bâton in the other !

Again and again Tchaikovsky's heart pressed the suit of opera upon a coldly rejective mind. A melancholy, lyrical temperament does not father great opera, and faint praise told him so whenever one reached production point. The first night would be a huge success—his reputation would ensure that. Then the applause would vanish like a blown-out candle. Of compromises there were plenty : ballet music, suites (do not forget the *Casse Noisette*, though even that was coldly received by the Russian public), musical accompaniments to dramatic action. In any work where the music had not to be integral with the idea of the drama, Tchaikovsky was successful. He could paint atmosphere, but not character in music—no character, that is, except his own. At that he showed an increasing grasp and facility which finally stamped him as a master of mourning. Yet he never lost his infatuation for opera, and there is much wistfulness in the thought of a man whose triumph was to be the revelation of his own soul, striving after that will-o'-the-wisp, the exposition of the souls of others. Typical, too, of that strange perversity was it that Mozart was his favourite composer, that the first musical love of his life, when he was a careless and unambitious student qualifying for a Government clerkship in the School of Jurisprudence, should have been Italian opera. Both influences persisted in the texture of his later works, and gave them a flavour of sombre gaiety, so that we can say of Tchaikovsky more than of any other composer, that his sincerest laughter with some pain is fraught. In his greatest moments he reaches humanity through the dark street where all blinds are drawn and every ear listens for the hearse.

The first measure of real freedom he had known came to him at the Villa Maidonovo, and he took advantage of it to act as a kind of presiding deity. He instituted a routine as strict as the rising and setting of the sun, including the two-hour afternoon walk which the villagers came to know so well. As his fame spread, so did his spirit withdraw. He became secretive about his compositions, cultivated few friends and made the rest unwelcome. He was marshalling his energies for a great assault on the public, under his own supervision. The first awakening of interest in public affairs was parochial—he took a leading part in the establishment of a school for the village children, whom he considered were unduly idle—probably he had an eye to quieter walks. Thus he rusticated for two years, and in his retirement many honours were paid him. He had dedicated twelve songs to the Empress, and she returned the compliment with the gift of an autograph portrait. On an excursion to the Caucasus he was crowned by brother composers with a silver wreath. Everything about him made for happiness, yet he was not happy. Life at Maidonovo began to sicken him. He longed for action and began a triumphant tour of the capitals of Central Europe, met Brahms, Grieg and Dvorak, and recorded that in London he was recalled three times, 'which means a great deal from the reserved London public'. Returning from the tour, he made a new home at Frovloskoe, not far from his old one, and settled down to finish his *Fifth Symphony*. But a devil of restlessness was upon him, an incubus which was henceforth to haunt him until the end of his days. In less than a year's time he plunged into a riot of public engagements, toured, conducted the Jubilee Festival of his old teacher, Anton Rubinstein, and then, almost exhausted by exertions which another composer would have taken in his stride but which were novel to him, he retired to Italy to work on his new opera, *Queen of Spades*.

As always, he declared that he had at last found the ideal subject. St Petersburg did not think so when it was given there in 1890. That might have upset him had not a far greater sorrow loomed in his path. His 'dear, kind, incomparable friend', Nadejda, suddenly cut off the allowance she had made him for thirteen years, with the excuse that she was on the brink of ruin. Tchaikovsky replied with a letter full of expressions of gratitude and sympathy. Immediately afterwards he heard that her affairs had been righted. To a nature like Tchaikovsky's the sudden recovery was full of significance. It was, he declared, an attempt to get rid of him on the first opportunity. From then on he regarded their friendship as ' a commonplace, silly joke, which fills me with disgust and shame '. The blow left him with a scar which he carried to the grave. His last delirium was full of reproaches directed to the faithless friend.

With such an event were initiated the years of the *Pathetic Symphony*, the work which, above all others, was to submit the decision of Tchaikovsky's fame, not only to contemporary Europe, but to posterity as well. There were no lack of episodes to confirm in him the mood which set in upon the news of Nadejda's dereliction. Not long before he had lost his old friend Hubert, and his favourite niece, Vera Rimsky-Korsakov. Then, on the eve of a tour in America, he learnt accidentally of the death of his favourite sister who, in the troubled days of his youth, had given him the run of her estate in which to find the peace which the city denied him. On his way to America he found he was not cut out for seafaring. He was seasick. The siren, ' a machine which emits a hideous roar, like a gigantic tiger ', got on his nerves. The tour was successful, but Tchaikovsky was not the man to believe that one ray of sunshine makes a summer. He settled again, in yet another new house near Klin, and began work on the Symphony.

Into it he poured all his essential nature, transferring from opera the whole of his belief that he was writing a masterpiece. He was to miss the world's applause by a few weeks and to go to his grave thinking it had failed, for when he conducted the performance at St Petersburg in October, 1893, the orchestra was indifferent and the applause very moderate. A few days later Tchaikovsky took to his bed. Cholera was diagnosed, and he faced his end with calm before drifting into a delirium only ended by death, unilluminated by the knowledge that had he lived a month or two longer he would have heard his last symphony take Europe by storm.

So this son of an inspector of mines wandered out of life as he had wandered through it, missing by the merest margin the reward of an achievement towards which he had struggled blindly for thirty years, since that critical time when he had, after a careless adolescence, rejected clerkship and given his soul to music and his body to poverty. Into the unknown he followed a trail of friends, Zvierev, Kondratiev—by whose deathbed at Aix he experienced heart-rendering emotions—and Apukhtin, the poet. All Russia, from the Emperor downwards, mourned him. Among the friends he left, to more particular grief, were Anton Rubinstein, his early teacher, whom all his life he reverenced but who returned his devotion with a scarcely concealed contempt for his brilliant pupil's work. Tchehov, too, who had honoured him with the dedication of a book. Laroche, another of those who had helped him in his youth and pained him by criticism of his mature work. Pained, but not alienated; for Tchaikovsky always took criticism heroically, perhaps because he did not pay much attention to it. He would accept dogma on everything except his music, and there he claimed to be the supreme, the final, Judge. Terribly he nurtured in himself the Miltonic dictum : ' The mind is its own place. . . .' He found that, left to its own conclusions untempered by outside influences, it is more likely to make a hell of heaven than a heaven of hell. But, fighting magnificently through the smoke and flame of his own temperament to the clear levels of symphonic tragedy, he at last came to grips with the sombre implications of his own spirit and exorcised them with a master-stroke which ranks him with Brahms, Mozart and Beethoven. After a lifetime's tussle with Quantity he achieved through a thickening haze of suffering that Quality which, however small its vessel, irrevocably places its author in that select region where comparison is frivolous and criticism irrelevant. Tchaikovsky died short of universal fame, but within him must have been the song of the Archangels driving Satan from Paradise.

XIV

VERDI

By HERMON OULD

IN 1813 the village of Le Roncole, seventeen miles north-west of Parma, in Italy, was invaded by the Austrians and Russians, who pillaged, destroyed, sacked, and massacred. The villagers rushed hither and thither for safety, and a group of terrified women sought refuge in the church, where, protected by the image of the Virgin, they imagined they would be safe. But the soldiers forced their way into the church; women and children were slaughtered, and the church became a shambles. One woman, with a child at her breast, fled to the belfry and hid there, sick with terror, until the marauders had gone. The woman was the mother of Verdi; the child, Verdi himself.

If those psychologists are right who claim that it is only the impressions made before one's tenth year that radically affect the character, this episode is not without its importance; and another incident, which occurred seven years later, may be credited with a share in the development of a composer whose work is the most dramatic in musical history. More than a hundred years ago, Giuseppe Verdi, then a small boy of seven, was an acolyte, attached to the village church. A serving-boy at Mass must have his wits about him. The ritual, even in a village church, is fairly elaborate, and an acolyte in attendance on a priest must be ready to genuflect at the right times, retire into obscurity when necessary, and 'serve' water at the appropriate moments. Young Verdi was a serious child, given to day-dreaming, and one day during Mass his mind was carried away from his duties by the music which came from the organ. To the sensitive child it appeared to be almost divine, and at the elevation of the Host, the solemnest moment in the celebration of Mass, it was most entrancing of all.

The priest turned to the boy. 'Water', he demanded in a whisper; but young Verdi's spirit was elsewhere. 'Water!' repeated the priest, agitated and annoyed. But the boy's attention was concentrated on the organ. The priest was aghast. 'Water!' he said for the third time, and gave the dreaming acolyte a surreptitious but forceful kick which sent him headlong down the steps of the altar. Unconscious, the boy was carried into the vestry . . . and presumably he was a better acolyte thenceforward. All we know for certain is that when he regained consciousness he pleaded with his father to allow him to learn music. And that was how Verdi, in his eighth year, came to possess a spinet which remained with him till he died.

Verdi's life as a composer may be said to have begun when, exploring the possibilities of his spinet, he discovered the major third and fifth of the key of C. This was like a heavenly revelation, and the memory of it stayed with him through the night. Next day he sought eagerly to repeat the experience, but however he manipulated the keys, he could not find the same combination of notes. In a fit of anger, he seized a hammer and began to belabour the poor instrument until his father caught him at it and suitably chastised him. Doubtless it was after suffering this maltreatment that the spinet was given to a local instrument-maker to repair; and the following inscription on one of the 'jacks' is a testimony both to the youthful Verdi and to the perspicacious spinet-maker :—

'This I do gratis in consideration of the good disposition the boy Giuseppe Verdi shows in learning to play on this instrument, which quite satisfies me for any trouble. Signed: Stephen Cavaletti, A.D. 1821.'

This record of violence is by no means typical of Verdi, whose disposition seems to have been outwardly calm, gentle and reserved, however fiery he may have been within. From the time when his musical aptitude was discovered by an old itinerant fiddler named Bagasset, who used to play outside the inn kept by Verdi's father, music absorbed him to the exclusion of most other things. We like romantically to think of musical geniuses fighting against discouragement during their early life, but Verdi would not serve as a good example of the cussedness of Fate. Considering the circumstances in which he was born—son of a poor chandler and innkeeper—it is surprising that his talent was so quickly recognized and so carefully fostered. By the age of ten he had finished his education and was engaged as an office boy by one Antonio Barezzi, the head of a large wholesale grocery business in Busseto, and, what is more to the point, President of the local Philharmonic Society. He kept a shrewd and kindly eye on young Verdi, who was not only allowed to attend the rehearsals of the Philharmonic Society, but spent most of his time copying out orchestral parts. He actually received instruction from the conductor of the orchestra, Giovanni Provesi, who at the end of two years declared that the child knew as much as he did himself.

' He will go far, and one day become a great master ! ' declared Provesi. From the age of eleven the boy was organist at Le Roncole, and when he was sixteen he wrote numerous pieces (now in the archives of Busseto) for the Philharmonic Society. When he was eighteen he was given a bursary by the Monte di Pieta of 600 francs a year for two years to enable him to study in Milan, and the good Barezzi made himself answerable for board and other expenses. But the Conservatoire in Milan did not want him, the Director, Francesco Basily, saying that the youth showed no musical disposition. Two years later Basily and the famous teacher, Lavigna, were discussing the result of a competition for the post of organist, for which twenty-eight musicians had applied and had failed to develop correctly a theme supplied by Basily.

' I wager Verdi would have done better than your twenty-eight ', said Lavigna. Verdi was called and given the task. He not only accomplished it but threw in a double canon on the subject. ' Why ? '

asked Basily. ' I found it rather poor and wished to embellish it ', answered Verdi, getting his own back. Not that he was commonly given to retaliation. Although often the centre of conflict, he seldom engaged in it.

Thus it was when, on the death of Giovanni Provesi, everybody assumed that Verdi would succeed him as choirmaster and organist of the collegiate foundation, as well as chief director of the Philharmonic Society. The clergy were against Verdi, ostensibly on account of the secular character of his work, and put forward a mediocre organist, one Giovanni Ferrari, in opposition. Being recommended by two bishops, Ferrari was elected, and this was the beginning of a deadly feud between the Philharmonic Society, supported by Barezzi, and the clerical party. There followed ' outrages, insults, satires, and strife of all kinds, which were the cause of imprisonments, persecutions, and other annoyances.'

But Verdi remained aloof. He was now beginning to feel his feet as a composer; his ambition was developing, and he was in love with Berezzi's eldest daughter, Margherita, who, we are told, was ' taking and clever.' She returned his love and her father had so much respect and affection for Verdi that he consented to the marriage, although the twenty-three-year-old composer was practically penniless. In 1836 they were married; within two years a boy and a girl were born to them; in 1838 Verdi was appointed to the conductorship of the Milan Philharmonic Society; and in 1839 his first opera was produced.

And now once more Verdi was to be the centre of a drama. Bartolomeo Merelli, the impresario of La Scala opera house in Milan, impressed by Verdi's work, commissioned three operas. At the time Verdi was ill in bed with throat trouble and worried about money. Rent was overdue and he was on the point of appealing to his father-in-law for money when this commission came. He sent Merelli a request for an advance, but the message did not reach him; no money came, and Verdi's wife was forced to sell some of her jewels. Then the little boy was taken ill suddenly, and died in the heartbroken mother's arms. Almost immediately afterwards the daughter fell ill and died; and less than two months later Verdi's wife was stricken with ' brain fever ' and passed away.

' I was alone! alone! ' he writes, ' and in the midst of this terrible anguish, to avoid breaking the engagement I had contracted, I was compelled to write and finish a comic opera! '

The ' comic opera ' was entitled *Un Giorno di Regno*. It was produced at the Scala and was a failure. It was the only comic opera he ever wrote, if we except his masterpiece, *Falstaff*. He decided to give up composition, and begged Merelli to cancel his agreement. Whereupon Merelli said—and the words are worth recording *pour encourager les autres* : ' Listen, Verdi, I can't force you to write; but my confidence in you is not shaken. Give me two months' notice before the beginning of a season and I promise that any opera you bring shall be put on the stage.'

Verdi clung to his determination for a year and

then, his need for expression being stronger than his will, he wrote another opera, almost under protest. This was called *Nabucco*, and although it created a furore when it was produced in Italy and was a popular success in England, it is now all but forgotten. Indeed, Verdi's early operas, with the possible exception of *Ernani*, would have secured him scarcely more than honourable mention in the history of opera. True son of Italy, his gift for melody would have passed unremarked, being no more noteworthy than similar gifts possessed by his immediate predecessors and contemporaries—Bellini, Donizetti, Rossini; and it was not until he entered upon his 'second period' with *Rigoletto* that his place in the history of music became assured. The production of *Rigoletto* established the composer for good in the eyes of the musical world, that and the two operas which followed, *Il Trovatore* and *La Traviata*. After the spectacular horrors, blood, splendour, madness and hysteria of which most operas of the time were compact, the quiet story of *Traviata* (based on the younger Dumas' 'La Dame aux Camélias') must have seemed revolutionary, and its first production in Italy was indeed a fiasco, finishing amidst uncontrolled laughter. Verdi himself wrote to one of his best friends the day after the performance: '*La Traviata* last night was a failure. Was the fault mine or the singers'? Time will judge.' The laughter was due to the incongruity of the casting. Donatelli, who played the part of the consumptive heroine, was enormously stout, and the audience simply would not believe in her imminent demise.

Although Verdi shunned publicity, he became the idol of Italy and was held up as a symbol of Italian patriotism. Even his name was regarded superstitiously as representing: 'Viva *V*ittorio *E*mmanuele *R*e *D'I*talia' (Long live Victor Emanuel, King of Italy), and every first performance of his operas was in the nature of a political demonstration. True to his character, Verdi took no active part in all this excitement, but he was known to be intensely patriotic.

In his old age he retired to his estate at Sant' Agata and lived the life of a country gentleman, farming, breeding horses, and so forth, and no further work of importance was expected of the composer of *Aïda*. But on November 1, 1886, when Verdi was seventy-three years of age, he completed a work which was incomparably finer than anything he had written before, *Otello*, which showed that his mind was as youthful as ever and his technical skill unimpaired. Six years later, then in his eightieth year, he gave to an astonished world the greatest of all his operas, *Falstaff*, based on Shakespeare's *Merry Wives of Windsor*. The agility, robustiousness and humour; the technical dexterity, the subtle characterization, the humanity and inventiveness of this work of an old man are remarkable and a happy climax to a fruitful life. Nothing of note came from his pen after *Falstaff*. On the morning of January 21, 1901, a servant observed him trying to do up a button; his fingers fumbled and the servant offered to help him. 'What does it matter, one button more or less?' asked Verdi. He sank to the ground, and never regained consciousness.

Italy would have loved to attend the funeral of this master of melody with the pomp and ceremony appropriate to a man who had added so much to Italy's glory; but he had asked for a quiet burial, at sunset or at sunrise, and requested that there should be no cards, no flowers—and no music ! The request is not out of keeping with his way of living. The man who in his work had called up the glories of ancient Egypt, the Hanging Gardens of Babylon, the trappings of the Renaissance, was, in his own life, unpretentious, modest, undramatic. When he became famous decorations were showered upon him. The King of Italy elected him a senator, but he never once attended a sitting. He was even made a member of parliament for Busseto, but it was not long before he resigned. As he grew rich his generosity became a by-word, and there is no space here even to mention the recorded instances of it. The institution of Monte di Pieta, which had granted him a bursary as a boy, was handsomely rewarded; his benefactor Barezzi was repaid, and the old fiddler Bagasset was not forgotten.

XV
WAGNER
By RICHARD CHURCH

I WONDER if it is possible to discuss the man behind the music without having something to say about that music. For what is any man, and most particularly a creative artist, apart from his achievement? He is a mere passage-way, through which the creatures of his imagination have come and gone, leaving only an echo of their voices and a ghostly remembrance of their hopes and fears, their passions, and their mental dignity. It is, therefore, as unfair as it is unreal to try to picture the man without his work. When we see a concentration of light we look behind it for the burning-glass by which it is focused. The light is the work, the man is the lens, and the source of supply is the sun of truth and beauty, which is named according to the race and religion of the onlooker.

We are concerned with the man Wagner, but some idea of his personality can be given only to a reader whose feeling for great music will be expressed in these happy sentences by Sir Hubert Parry: ' Not only is it really worth while to make a little effort to appreciate what is first-rate, but in point of fact it is only the object of getting nearer to understanding and feeling what is thoroughly good and noble that makes art worth taking any trouble about at all. The silly sipping of one sweet after another, and passing day after day from one ephemeral piece of elegance to another, just to make acquaintance with a new sensation, or get through an hour which might otherwise hang heavy on the hands, is utterly unworthy of the dignity of a human being.'

Similarly, in our effort to appreciate the grandeur and force of Wagner's vitality, we must try to realize what were the conditions, of environment and inheritance, under which he fought. Only then can we grasp the many-sidedness of his conquest and the volatility and strength of character by which that conquest was made possible.

In one respect he was fortunate, for he came at a propitious moment in the history of dramatic music. For a hundred years this branch of the art had been drooping. Its first promise at the end of the seventeenth century, when Carissimi and Monteverde were laying the foundations of opera on a right dramatic base, had been betrayed. In the marriage of music and poetry the latter had become an uxorious drudge in order that music, the bride, might indulge her vanity. To this purpose, truth of idea and all dramatic development were sacrificed until opera was reduced to a stilted formula upon which were hung florid trills and arias to suit the vocal organs of individual virtuosi. Lulli in France and Scarlatti in Italy did something towards restoring a right relationship; but how far they failed we may see by the hard struggle which awaited Gluck, whom we may call the parent of that form of opera which was to admit of development in the direction of the music-drama born a century later out of Wagner's genius. After Gluck, the artificiality returned, and composers who had something original to express gave up opera in despair. Even Beethoven could do little with it. He stumped about in it like a farmer in a perfumery shop. The tradition had become so set that no poet ever thought of collaborating with a composer, and the latter had to go for his libretti to mere hacks, whom he treated as such, as we see, for instance, from Mozart's letters.

Even with these unhealthy conditions, however, opera was beginning to show signs of new life under the dynamic energy of Berlioz (who wrote his own libretti), and the native grace of Weber. Then in addition, Meyerbeer, a vulgar fellow with an indolent spirit, brought a certain *loosening*, though very theatrical force, into the structure of the musical idiom in its relation to the dramatic subject.

Such was the state of the field when Wagner came to plough it. He found it full of tares and broken masonry, and it bristled with conservative landlords and gamekeepers. He was not unprepared, for from childhood he was acquainted with, and had an instinct for, the theatre.

He was the youngest of nine children, born in 1813 to a studious civil servant in Leipzig. An intimate friend of the family was one Ludwig Geyer, a Jewish actor and dramatist, and a kind, sensitive man. It has been suggested that *he* was Wagner's father, and handed on the dramatic talent. Whether this be true or not, he became the boy's step-father when Richard was two, and guided the next eight years of his life, before departing into the grave, leaving the family to exist precariously in Dresden.

We know that the child was precocious, both mentally and nervously. He learned Latin and Greek quickly, and at fourteen taught himself English in order to read Shakespeare. Under the influence of this disturbing poet, he attempted a grand tragedy of his own, the cast for which consisted of his admiring sisters, three of whom were to become actresses later in life. At this time Weber's *Der Freischütz* was produced in Dresden, and the boy thus found another mentor. He proceeded to put his tragedy to music.

His nervous development was equally remarkable. He had an abnormal sense of touch. Often he would creep into his sisters' rooms when the young women were out, so that he might rub his cheeks against the silks and satins hanging in the wardrobes. The prickly smoothness of the material and the scent of the feminine perfume lingering therein would make the boy tremble and burst into tears: a kind of emotional or sensuous inebriation to which he was prone all his life. As an old man he would drape himself in silken or velvet cloaks in order to stimulate certain emotional reactions which would move him to composition.

Following the first demonstration of musical ability, his mother put him for six months under the excellent teacher Weinlich. Apart from this instruction, which he took none too graciously, he was practically self-taught. By the time he was twenty he had made himself intimate, in detail, with Beethoven's nine symphonies, and under their inspiration wrote one for himself. This was performed in Leipzig, but attracted no attention. One has to remember that from certain points of view he was always an amateur; earnest, naive, enthusiastic; entering where the angels of professionalism feared to tread. All these qualities are characteristic of the self-taught amateur working in solitude. But it is from such sources that so much of the most sublime work of mankind emerges. To be sublime, to attempt the heroic, one has to be innocent of the rules and the pitfalls which make the experts shiver with apprehension. Think of old Leukenhoeve with his optical glasses, of the youth Adams who discovered the planet Neptune, of Colonel Lawrence, the amateur soldier. As Professor Tovey says, 'more than a modicum of rusticity is needed as a protection to a man who attempts colossal reforms'. The virtues of that quality of rusticity Wagner never lost; the freshness, the fearlessness, and the simplicity. It must not be overlooked, however, that with them, and giving them utility, there went an immense facility in acquiring technique, a comprehensive memory, and that feminine intuition—so characteristic of genius—for culling the important blossoms from the widest possible field of knowledge. Wagner's intellectual hunger was insatiable, and when he was not engaged in composition of music or stage sets, he was either reading—principally in philosophy or the Greek dramatists—or studying the scores of the great masters of the past. This last practice, indulged at so influential a time in his life, gave his work an orthodox sub-structure and a firm root in historical form, without which it could never have carried its huge polyphonic growth, that massive impressionism which seems to be more revolutionary in appearance than it is in fact.

These activities prevented Wagner from becoming an instrumentalist, though they made him such a master of the orchestra that his conducting of the Beethoven *Ninth Symphony* was the first to make that superb work popular.

When he was twenty-one he was appointed Music Director of the theatre at Magdeburg. This post was held for two years, during which time he produced his opera *Das Liebesverbot*, founded on Shakespeare's *Measure for Measure*. It was too much for so provincial a group of artists, and the performance was a failure. One of the company, Minna Planer, a pretty but somewhat depressing woman of pedestrian intelligence but a faithful heart, consoled the disappointed musician, and he married her in 1836 at Riga, where he had obtained another appointment. In his 'Life,' he says very naively that the officiating priest, after the ceremony, spoke of One who was coming into their lives with repeated help. The unhappy couple—for Wagner was very depressed about the prospects of his work—construed this as meaning that a patron was at hand who would subsidize the composer. When they learned that the priest's allusion was purely conventional, the violent young egoist was enraged and practical-minded Minna in tears. This story illustrates Wagner's extraordinary selfless egoism, if one may use such a paradox. He absorbed everything and everybody into the consummation of his life-work, that purpose which began more and more patiently to cohere as he gained practical experience in the theatre. He knew that he had to bring opera back to its first happy form, but with the importation of the vast inheritance of pure music which had accumulated during the intervening century and a half.

The energy for carrying on this accumulative task, however, was won at great expense. All who came to him had to *give*: time, money, brains, their very individual integrity. And so great was his power that most people were willing to sacrifice themselves and their ambitions to his necessity. Liszt, Bülow, the Devrients, the Wesendoncks, the King of Bavaria—all devoted themselves to his work, contributing their own power, influence, love, and wealth. The one exception was Nietzsche, who was too pronounced a being to play the lieutenant or connive at his own submersion.

Bülow, in particular, made a supreme sacrifice. His wife Cosima, Liszt's daughter, devastated Wagner's tempestuous heart just when he was at the very summit of his achievement. The *Ring* was in progress, *Tristan* was complete, and he was about to start *Die Meistersinger*. He was ill with erysipelas and nervous exhaustion; the theatre managers throughout Europe were frightened of the increasing originality of his work, and refused to produce it. He was in debt, due to one failure after another of concert schemes. The business side of life encroached upon his hours of work until they vanished. His passion for Cosima was consuming him. Bülow, Cosima, and Liszt talked over the situation, and the noble-hearted husband sacrificed himself without bitterness, retaining still his advocacy of Wagner's work, and conducting performances of it as often as possible. Cosima went to Wagner, and from that time—1870—until her recent death, she gave her life to him and his work. Many bitter things have been said about her, and of the eclipse of Minna; but I think the truth in this matter is to be found in Mr Ernest Newman's inferences in his *Life* of the master. Cosima was a woman of great beauty and force of character; a dominant spirit; and without her administrative ability and protecting power it is probable that Wagner would never have been able to gather up the many ramifications of his life-work into the magnificent unity which found expression at Bayreuth.

In a humbler, but no less sincere if less intelligent and conscious, way, Minna gave her service during the early years of Wagner's struggles. Following their marriage, they went to Paris in 1839, their only assets being a Newfoundland dog and the manuscript of *Rienzi*. Meyerbeer gave the young newcomer letters of introduction, but none of the sophisticated Paris managers would touch his opera. There followed a struggle for existence,

Minna took in lodgers, and blacked their boots. Wagner did hack work, arranging popular airs and operas for piano and cornet, correcting proof sheets, and writing articles for the musical papers. On some days he rose from his bed, moved to his chair, and did not leave it until he fell exhausted into bed late at night. Minna put his food beside him as he worked. In spite of this drudgery and discouragement, he gathered about him a circle of admirers, and also wrote both the book and the music of *The Flying Dutchman*. With all his cries of agony, his eternal railing at the world for its neglect of him, he stuck to his ideals.

Reward came through the production of *Rienzi* at Dresden in 1842. It was a success, and he was made conductor of the State Opera there. All might have gone well, in spite of the heavy duties entailed, had there not occurred in 1848 the feverish year of revolution which convulsed Europe. Naturally Wagner was on the side of freedom against officialdom; and as he was himself an official, things became awkward. He even addressed the mob from the barricades. The result was exile and flight to Paris. This part of his life has been told by Romain Rolland in the musical novel *John Christopher*.

Life was very black. Minna was losing heart, worn out by the high pace of this continual battle against a world now definitely hostile. Even Wagner was discouraged, and he wrote that ' I thought everything was at an end with my artistic creativeness'. However, Liszt was working for him at Weimar, and the rich Wesendoncks invited him to Zurich. There he lived in seclusion for six years, without composing a note, while he studied Schopenhauer, a philosopher whom he found had rationalized his own conception of the lofty position held by music among the arts. He also wrote on the theory of his art, and clarified the huge mass of experience gathered during his life. The result was a still more coherent purpose, and from this time until the end of his life he drove on without pause, until the vision was made palpable in the great tetralogy of the *Ring*, in *Tristan*, *Die Meistersinger*, and *Parsifal*.

As the edifice rose, disciples gathered round to defend it. Wagner became a king in this world of the mind, and his capital at Bayreuth has since been a Mecca for the faithful. As with most shrines whence the prophet has departed, the dust of habit and mediocre interpretation has begun to settle there, and at the moment the full power and fruition of Wagner's genius cannot be estimated at first hand, since they lack a physical demonstration that would have satisfied the master himself.

XVI

WEBER

By FRANCIS BRETTARGH

SO little of Weber's music is current that, though that little is infinitely precious and infinitely beloved, it is easy to forget how great a man he was. He died young, at the age of thirty-nine; but the poignancy of early death is not, as with a Mozart or a Schubert, a sense of power cut off in its prime, but rather of power unfulfilled even in his lifetime. He belonged to two worlds. He was born in the pre-Revolution world of classical ideals and patronage; he died in the post-Revolution world of independence and romanticism. His tragedy was that he could not adapt himself rapidly enough to the new conditions: he was a romantic held captive in an eighteenth-century court. For such the court of Dresden remained long after the fall of Napoleon.

German romanticism was born of her humiliations. It was stirring when Jena was fought and when the armies were marching to Moscow. It came to full birth at the downfall, with the wakening of a new national consciousness. It sought its inspiration in the history of the German peoples, in the tales of the heroes, in the legends of their forests and rivers. Weber's nature was dramatic, and to him in the early 'twenties these things came like a wind of inspiration. They drove his music into a closer alliance with the other arts, towards the direct expression of emotion, so that it must borrow the terms of poetry and painting to describe itself. In opera, to which he was drawn by temperament and training, they inspired that attempt to reflect in music not only the characters but the colour and incidents of the story: the first step towards the fusion of drama and music which Wagner fulfilled. They inspired also the choice of subjects in which the mysterious, the elfin, or the romantic predominated. He too thrilled to ' the velvet and bright iron of the past '. With Weber it is like finding oneself at the source of a great river. To him one traces so many beginnings. One finds music learning to walk hand in hand with literature, dependent upon and inspired by it; the musician becomes reader and then writer himself; he becomes critic. In this respect also Weber is the forerunner of Schumann and Liszt and Berlioz.

Weber was born in 1786. He opened his eyes upon the painted world of make-believe. The greenroom was his nursery. He had the most enchanting toy-theatre imaginable, for it was life-sized. His family were, in effect, strolling players. Music and the stage were in their blood. A Baron von Weber in the early seventeenth century had owned his private theatre and orchestra, and though fortune stripped the family, this passion survived. Weber's father is an engaging figure: reckless, dilettante, bohemian, yet lovable. He gave Carl Maria no orthodox musical training, yet forced his talent by every means. He hoped the child might turn into a lucrative prodigy, as his cousin Mozart had been. By the age of twelve Carl Maria had written his first opera ; by eighteen, two others, and they were performed ; and at that incredible age we find him in charge of the opera at Breslau. An academic education upon classical lines could hardly have done more ; and it is to be supposed that he had the technique of the stage at his fingertips.

From his father and those wandering years Weber inherited qualities, good and ill, which made up, on the whole, a stern handicap. He had been a sickly child, with a disease of the hip-bone which left him lame. He was a slender figure, with long arms, and a thin, pale face. He was consumptive. His eyes were large and brilliant ; he had an enchanting smile. Aristocracy had bred in him great charm of manner; it had bred also those multifarious instincts that may best be described as a taste for income. His youth is a record of extravagance, of passionate and expensive amours, of soaring debts ; and in the matter of debts his father was the best of companions. His father—whom he loved so well and with whose care he had so early to saddle himself ! It would be interesting to trace the reactions which came into play as he grew older, swinging him so violently away from the earlier bohemianism ; and to discern the force at work, whether it was his art, or an atavism, or fears merely, or the encroachment of disease. The vagabond became the man impassioned of security: 'if only God will bestow on me some post without cares and with a salary on which a man can live!' The spendthrift grew into the man who at crippling sacrifice paid not only his own debts but his father's as well; and through more than one love affair, extravagant, unworthy, bitterly disillusioning, he was groping toward love, and found it in the most domestic of marriages. But domesticity would seem to be a note of German romanticism.

It was not until he was thirty that he came to anchor. There had been years of concert-touring —he was a considerable pianist—and he had spent three in Prague, finding out that it was one thing to conduct an opera, another to direct an opera season. The lesson he failed to learn, unhappily, was that a man sick as he has no place in an opera house. He found his haven in the court of Dresden. In the same year he married. It was far from being 'a post without cares'; and the salary was poor. Of the German courts, all of them staunch adherents of Italianism, Dresden was the staunchest. The King of Saxony had been a creature of Napoleon's. Things French and Italian were cherished in pious memory of their friend and ally; the new nationalism was suspect. Only grudgingly was a German theatre permitted a footing in Dresden. And Weber—was he not the minstrel of romanticism? Had he not set to music Körner's *Lyre and Sword*, those songs of a people's deliverance? In a little society where everything was ordered by the court, the king's prejudice was a serious obstacle. Weber had the greatest difficulty in getting a status for German opera, or for himself a rank equal to Morlacchi's, the Italian director. Morlacchi was the most accomplished of schemers, all-powerful, a favourite of the king's. Life at Dresden was an elaborate minuet. Weber found himself involved in an intricate pattern of petty observances and duties. Where he should have been voyaging to fairyland, minting into imperishable treasure the riches of his dreams, we find him in an awkward uniform conducting an interminable programme at an interminable banquet; or at the organ in the court chapel; or with Morlacchi's work to do as well as his own; or amid the dusty business of the theatre, the disputes, the intrigues, the jealousies, the incessant battling of the world of opera. When he came to Dresden he had not written the first of the works by which he is principally known; and *Der Freischütz*, when it was begun, was three years in the writing. It was upon this altar of sterile routine that Weber sacrificed the inheritance of posterity.

There is no doubt he was a fine director. In more than one way he recalls Liszt at Weimar. There was the same catholicity; the same generous search for new genius; the same singular *riposte* to the malevolence of rivals by giving a more than ordinarily careful performance of their music. He was infinitely painstaking: he learnt Czech at Prague in order to rehearse the Czech members of the company, and one of his last labours, when writing *Oberon*, was to learn English, so as to rehearse it in London. His performers adored him. We can picture him in the punctilious performance of the daily ritual, calling where calls had to be made, leaving flowers where flowers had to be left, remembering everyone's birthdays and anniversaries, in the good German fashion, and everyone's rank and title, a dapper little man—one can only call him dapper—in the blue frockcoat with the shiny buttons, the Hessian boots, the embroidered cravat, the tawny coat over his arm, the broad round hat: a familiar figure in the streets of Dresden.

Yet he was the loneliest of men. He yearned for friendship. And one must call him mercurial only because there is no stronger word. Gaiety and gloom chased each other like the black and white of an April day. Each mood seemed to him eternal. Most men in grey weather know that there is a sun. Weber could not even imagine one. His gaiety was never serene; it had the champagne-quality of the *Invitation à la Valse*. ' I reason myself by main force into a sort of contentment', he said once, ' but the naturally cheerful state of mind which steels all one's nerves and sends one's spirits bubbling up of themselves, *that* one cannot give oneself.' He was sensitive beyond words. His disease turned pricks into knife-wounds; he had no covering against criticism or apathy. The first night of *Der Freischütz* was the happiest hour of his life; when the news reached him that audiences in Vienna were cooling to *Euryanthe* his spirits sank to the grave. He looked for omens in everything. He believed himself to be watched by an Evil Star. ' My Star', he would say, ' will demand its tribute of sorrow and annoyance.' It is ironic that he should hold his star to blame only for the trivial misfortunes of his career and not for the real tragedies: Dresden instead of Berlin, when Berlin had been almost in his grasp; the nonentities whom fate threw in his way as librettists. He who deserved a Heine or a Yeats, found a Helmine von Chezy, a Planché. That two of his three chief operas should survive only in their preludes—surely a constellation was at work!

Der Freischütz was produced at Berlin in 1821 on June 14. Dresden at first would have none of it. To a few it was 'the most unmusical row that was ever roared upon a stage'; many critics abused it; but the people took it to their hearts, even as in later years the people of Munich took *Tannhäuser* to their hearts, in defiance of the critics. It fitted the mood of the hour. It was the first thoroughly German opera; more national than *Die Zauberflöte* or *Fidelio*; and it was the first romantic opera, satisfying German aspirations. And it caught the imagination of Europe: it was soon to receive the singular distinction of being played in three London theatres at the same time. *Euryanthe* followed, ordered for Vienna. In 1824, Kemble offered Weber a commission to write an opera for Covent Garden. Dared he accept it? He was, as he knew well, a dying man. The doctors offered him a few years' life if he ceased working; they promised death within months, possibly weeks, if he continued. He chose the latter. A single thought now possessed him: how he might leave provision for his wife. He plunged into Planché's impossible libretto and managed to finish the opera in little over a year. The subject of *Oberon* he had chosen himself : Weiland's fairy poem had long haunted him. He arrived in England in the March of 1826.

In England, every thought was for his wife. For her, in continual letters, he records his simple pleasure in the new sights : the princely appointments of the stage-coach, the Kentish gardens, the neatness of England, the elegant comfort of Sir George Smart's house—where there was even a bath-room ! Everyone was most kind ; numerous cards awaited him ; a celebrated firm had sent him a piano. He was excited by the wealth of London. He foresaw behind her grim façades the golden rooms in candle-light ; intimate little concerts ; private lessons at anything up to five guineas. Rossini had done as well. But alas ! He reckoned without his hosts—or without their daughters ! The flamboyance of a curled and scented Rossini might tempt young ladies to coax reluctant guineas from their papas ; the limping little man with the sunken cheeks and the feverish eyes had not the secret. English aristocracy thawed to the bravura of the son of a town-trumpeter ; it froze to the breeding of Carl Maria von Weber. He played one evening at Lord Hertford's. Gaunt House ! Was Becky Sharp present, one wonders, to be civil to him ? ' She always made a point of being conspicuously polite to the professional ladies and gentlemen who attended ' (' Hush ! Silence ! There is Pasta beginning to sing ! '). This evening all the stars of the opera were there. Doubtless they had arrived by a back staircase and languished in an ante-room till their turn came. Possibly they were roped off from the elect like the common people in the ballroom scene in *Figaro*. Weber played to the babel of seven hundred guests. He could hardly himself hear what he was playing. He was indifferent. He knew that his fee from my Lord Steyne would be thirty guineas.

In his letters home no hint escaped him of the disappointments he was suffering, or of the increasing toll upon his strength. He says that he is very content with his singers, when the company at Covent Garden were raw to a degree ; he makes light of the intolerable strain of rehearsals, of the concerts he was under contract to conduct, of the gargantuan dinner parties he was forced to attend. But no bravery could conceal his horror at a London fog—' this is a day to shoot oneself '— or the tragi-comic affair of the Epsom Races which took society out of Town on the afternoon of his benefit concert. Again, his Evil Star !

One would like to take leave of him as he stands on the stage of Covent Garden on the night of April 12. It is interesting that until that day calls upon the stage were unheard of in England. But the first night of *Oberon* demanded a precedent. In that most magical of preludes is the whole of Weber : ' horns of elfland ', heralds of romance on dream-ramparts blowing their challenge to youth. Their sound carried over the seas. Mendelssohn heard them in Berlin, Schumann in Zwickau ; in Dresden, in the dreams of another schoolboy shadowy visions stirred, Tannhäuser, Siegfried, Tristan ; in Paris, Hector Berlioz took heart for his battle with the pendants. One would like to think that to the shrunken figure, trembling, radiant, facing the thunder of an English audience there came in that moment some intuition of this.

From that day the details of his journey home absorbed him. He had finished his task and now the overmastering home-sickness might have its way. Over and over again he covered in imagination every mile of it. On the last night they carried him to his bedroom in Portland Place. He bade his host good-night and said 'Let me sleep.' On the morrow they went to call him. They knocked and then beat upon the door; but there was no answer.